ESPECIALLY FOR

....

FROM

....

DATE

....

Published by Barbour Books, an imprint of Barbour Publishing, Inc., P.O. Box 719, Uhrichsville, Ohio 44683, www.barbourbooks.com

Our mission is to publish and distribute inspirational products offering exceptional value and biblical encouragement to the masses.

 Member of the
Evangelical Christian
Publishers Association

Printed in China.

God, Grant Me
WISDOM

DEVOTIONAL PRAYERS
FOR FATHERS

Tim Baker

BARBOUR BOOKS
An Imprint of Barbour Publishing, Inc.

CONTENTS

1. Wisdom for My Family

PATIENCE WITH MY KIDS

*Therefore, as God's chosen people, holy and dearly loved,
clothe yourselves with compassion, kindness,
humility, gentleness and patience.*
COLOSSIANS 3:12

Dear Jesus, I love my kids. I marvel at their creativity, and I love their personalities. You've blessed me with amazing humans to live with, to find joy with, and to discover the world with. Thank You for making me their father, for gifting me with these souls to shepherd for Your kingdom.

Thank You for making each of my kids what You intended them to be. As they grow, give me compassion for them so that I will care for them the way You would. As they struggle, help me speak words of wisdom. When they succeed, give them the gift of celebration through me. And God, lead me to lift them up to You daily. I love You, and I thank You for loving my kids. Amen.

WISDOM AS I LEAD MY FAMILY

*All your children will be taught by the L*ORD*,
and great will be their peace.*
ISAIAH 54:13

God, give me the courage to be a model for my family of a life that pursues You. As I try to be a godly man, give me wisdom about Your Word so that I can lead them to Your living water. Help me teach them truth, so they can live rightly. Reading Your Word is easy, so remind me to open it with them. Praying to You is simple, too, so give me the courage to bow daily with them so we can offer our hearts to You.

Through these acts, create me into someone whose family can look to him not only as a physical father but also as a spiritual father. Thank You for increasing my family's faith as I simply walk in Your footsteps. Amen.

BEING JUST WITH MY FAMILY

*When all Israel heard the verdict the king had given,
they held the king in awe, because they saw that
he had wisdom from God to administer justice.*
1 Kings 3:28

God, You are aware of the struggles I sometimes have
with my kids. One hurts the other, and then they fight.
And then they come to me crying, complaining about
how one hurt the other. It happens often. . .sometimes
every hour. Honestly, it's tiring.

I love my kids, but the constant back-and-forth is
a source of aggravation. Their ongoing feuds make it
difficult for me to be a righteous father, and I often blow
up and yell at them. But more than that, I struggle with
knowing who the offender is. And when that happens,
I default to punishing them both.

God, give me wisdom to know how to best manage
my children's arguments. More than that, make me a wise
judge who knows how to best lead them and how to best
show them what Your righteous judgment is like. Amen.

PROVIDING FOR MY FAMILY

Anyone who does not provide for their relatives,
and especially for their own household,
has denied the faith and is worse than an unbeliever.
1 TIMOTHY 5:8

God, I'm often quick to tell people that You've given me everything, and yet I'm also quick to spend my money on my own desires.

I know You've called me to give, so give me the strength to be a giver—especially to my family. Allow me the privilege of supporting my family with Your gifts. Make me a son who supports, a husband who provides, and a father who showers gifts on his children. Help me steward the money You have given me, and help me place it in the hands You'd place it in. Take away my desire to be selfish and give me a passion to surrender. Thank You for the opportunity to take what's in Your hands and place it in the hands of others. Amen.

LOVING MY WIFE

In this same way, husbands ought to love their wives as their own bodies. He who loves his wife loves himself.
EPHESIANS 5:28

God, each day I wake up next to the woman You called me to marry. I know her well—maybe *too* well. I know how she dresses, and I have her laugh memorized. I know what makes her angry and am all too aware that I push her buttons more often than I should. I know what frustrates her, but I often act carelessly, raising her frustration level.

I sometimes act like my wife's arch-nemesis, and it often feels like our relationship is filled with combat and not with love. I don't want it to be that way, God, so make me a man who loves his wife at all times, no matter what's happening in our marriage. When we're not getting along as well as we should, keep me from fueling the fire of anger. And in every moment, help me to love her the way You love me. And help us both grow to a deeper understanding of Your love for both of us. Amen.

PRAISING MY WIFE

Her children arise and call her blessed;
her husband also, and he praises her.
PROVERBS 31:28

Thanks, God, for my amazing wife. Her beauty often catches me off guard, and her spirit lifts me daily. Each day, she blesses the family by doing things without complaint. She never hesitates to make breakfast for me and lunch for the kids. But more than all that, Jesus, I see in my wife the selflessness that You lived here on earth. I see in her a Christ-like spirit that helps lead my family to follow You.

As my wife demonstrates what it means to be Your servant, help me to follow her example. When we're with our kids, help me to speak words that build her up. When we're with friends, prevent me from cutting her down. As we live life together, make me her biggest champion, her biggest fan, and the protector she needs. I know that the more I do these things, the more our children will catch on and imitate my actions.

Thank You, God, for the love You've given me for my wife. Amen.

ROMANCING MY WIFE

*Your lips drop sweetness as the honeycomb, my bride;
milk and honey are under your tongue. The fragrance
of your garments is like the fragrance of Lebanon.*
SONG OF SOLOMON 4:11

God, please help me to build romance back into my
marriage. Create in our relationship a sense of awe
and wonder for each other so that we are giddy with
excitement when we are together. Help us carve out time
to date each other and reconnect like we did when we
were younger. Remind me to buy her gifts, take her
to her favorite places, compliment her in front of others,
and say sweet things to her when we're alone. And most
of all, help me to treat her with the honor due Your child.
Thank You for the gift of my wife. Amen.

WISDOM TO BE A GODLY PARENT

*Moses listened to his father-in-law
and did everything he said.*
Exodus 18:24

Lord, parenting would be so much easier if I'd been given an instruction manual for how to handle difficult situations—like a crying baby at 3 a.m., like emotional late-night moments when my daughters need to vent, and like when I need to deal with my son's aggressive behavior.

Though I sometimes wish my kids had come with such a manual, I'm still grateful that You've made good advice available to me, grateful for those I know who serve as wise council, and grateful for the sages who have led me through some tough parenting moments.

Give me Your wisdom as I continue to lovingly parent my kids. Guide me by Your Holy Spirit so that I may raise them to know You and Your Word. Give me courage to make hard decisions, compassion to listen to them, and wisdom to guide them in love. Make me a good steward of their souls. Amen.

ENTRUSTING MY CHILDREN TO OTHERS

*"So now I give him to the LORD.
For his whole life he will be given over to
the LORD." And he worshiped the LORD there.*
1 SAMUEL 1:28

God, thank You for the example Hannah set in being willing to leave her child with Eli. I can't imagine how difficult it must have been for her to allow someone else to raise her baby boy. It was only through her amazing faith in You that she was able do such a thing.

I don't have too many Elis in my life, but I still need the kind of faith Hannah had. And I need other men in my life who can help me to raise my kids, men who can teach my kids things I cannot.

Help me to find friendships that will nourish me and also provide safe spaces for my kids. I don't intend to leave my kids in the care of others, but I want them to know other men who will help them understand what it means to be a grown person who seeks You with all their heart. Amen.

RELYING ON THE HOLY SPIRIT

"But the Advocate, the Holy Spirit, whom the Father will send in my name, will teach you all things and will remind you of everything I have said to you."
JOHN 14:26

God, though I don't fully understand what Your Spirit is like, how He operates, and what He does, I do know that I need Him in order to be the kind of husband and father You've called me to be.

When I read the New Testament, I see people who understood the power of Your Spirit and who did amazing things for Your kingdom through His empowerment. When I read of these people, I think: *What if I trusted Your Spirit as much as I trust in my job? What if I relied on Your Spirit as much as I rely on my paycheck? What if I followed the leading of Your Spirit as closely as I follow my favorite sports team?*

God, transform my present understanding of You into a deep reliance on the power of Your Spirit. I want to be a husband and father who lives and breathes by the moving of Your Spirit in my life. Amen.

2. Wisdom to Speak the Right Words

SPEAKING THE WORDS OF GOD

If anyone speaks, they should do so as one who speaks the very words of God. If anyone serves, they should do so with the strength God provides, so that in all things God may be praised through Jesus Christ. To him be the glory and the power for ever and ever. Amen.

1 PETER 4:11

Lord, each day I encounter friends who need to hear Your truth. In my conversations with these people, help me to be Your voice. Give me courage to speak the truth. When I speak, help me to remember that I am speaking Your words. Give me not only Your eyes to see where people are in life, but also Your thoughts so that I may encourage those I know need to move forward in their walk with You.

God, I know that Your words are true and that everything You speak leads me to eternal life. I have so many opportunities to listen for Your voice. Help me find the space in my schedule to first be a listener. Then give me the courage to follow Your Spirit's leading—and to speak the words He instructs me to speak. Amen.

SPEAKING THOUGHTFULLY, NOT RECKLESSLY

The words of the reckless pierce like swords,
but the tongue of the wise brings healing.
PROVERBS 12:18

God, so often I speak hastily. My words come out of my mouth too quickly, and too often without consideration for how they affect others. I often don't think about what I am saying, and I can be reckless with my words. In that recklessness, I often hurt those I love by speaking harsh words. Give me the wisdom Abraham had when he divided the land with Lot. Give me the wisdom Moses had when he spoke to Pharaoh. Give me the wisdom Peter had when he preached. Make me a man whose words bring healing. Instead of tearing others down, let me speak words that bring comfort and hope. Amen.

WORDS OF HEALING

Gracious words are a honeycomb,
sweet to the soul and healing to the bones.
PROVERBS 16:24

God, I have so many friends who are stuck in their brokenness. Their families are barely hanging together and their marriages are slowly dissolving. They're unhappy in their jobs, and their lives seem so pointless.

I know I'm not perfect in my speech, but help me to bring healing with my words. Where there is brokenness, help me bring wholeness. Where there is purposelessness, help me offer direction. Above all, give me courage to walk into broken moments where the lives of those I love are falling apart and be Your voice for their healing. Help me speak Your loving words to them, words that move them closer to Your kingdom. Amen.

LOVING WORDS

If I speak in the tongues of men or of angels,
but do not have love, I am only a
resounding gong or a clanging cymbal.
1 CORINTHIANS 13:1

God, it's so easy for me to criticize. It seems that I have a unique skill for unleashing mean-spirited and hurtful words. Simply said, God, I know how to use words to tear people apart.

Despite my keen ability to hurt others with my words, that's not my heart's desire. I love others and want to build them up. Make my words match my passion for others. Give me the words to encourage, not tear apart; the words to lift up, not shoot down.

I want to be known as a man who always encourages and always lifts others up. Make me that man, Lord, and help others to see the changes You've made in the way I use my words. Amen.

TRUTHFUL WORDS

*Instead, speaking the truth in love, we will
grow to become in every respect the mature
body of him who is the head, that is, Christ.*
EPHESIANS 4:15

God, I know You are truth, that there is nothing false
in You. Everything You say and everything You are 100
percent true.

Because You love me, You want me to hear truth
even when it stings. Help me to be a man who is willing
to hear Your truth. Don't allow my human need to be in
control get in the way of hearing Your words.

Help me seek out friends who will be honest with
me, who will have the courage to tell me the truth about
myself, my actions, and attitudes. Help me to graciously
receive words from those closest to me, and help me use
the guidance they offer me. Amen.

SPEAKING JUST WORDS

The mouths of the righteous utter wisdom,
and their tongues speak what is just.
PSALM 37:30

God, though my desire is to always speak what is just in Your eyes, it's not always easy speaking that way to *some* people. I struggle with telling that kind of truth to friends who don't make good decisions, and I don't like speaking words of justice to guys who are louder than I am, more opinionated than I am, or, frankly, bigger than I am.

But I've learned from watching the life of Jesus that He never struggled with speaking just words. When He heard or saw an injustice, He spoke about Your truth—no matter how formidable the opponent. God, make me like Christ. Give me courage to speak out Your justice. Help me to be honest with every man I meet, no matter how big or opinionated he may be. And, above all, make me the kind of man who is concerned first with honoring You with my words. Amen.

WORDS OF ENCOURAGEMENT

He traveled through that area,
speaking many words of encouragement
to the people, and finally arrived in Greece.
ACTS 20:2

Lord, the apostle Paul is an amazing example of the kind of man I want to become. He wasn't afraid to tell people the truth about You. He wasn't afraid of rulers, of angry crowds, or of people holding rocks. When people in positions of authority confronted him, he always seemed to have the right words. And in almost every situation, Paul had the special ability to encourage believers.

I want that ability God—the ability to speak words of encouragement. I want to speak the right words to defend Your kingdom and to encourage others to learn more about You. Make me like Paul, and make me ready to travel for You, speaking words of encouragement wherever I go. Amen.

SPEAKING WORDS OF BLESSING

While the whole assembly of Israel was standing there,
the king turned around and blessed them.
1 Kings 8:14

God, I'm not a king. I don't have the power of a president
or the ability to control an entire country. My decisions
don't affect a whole nation. However, people look to me
to lead them, and I want to be able to speak words that
bless every one of them.

Give me words of blessing for those I'm closest to—
words that build them up and help them understand Your
passion for them and for their future. Give me words that
help others understand Your dream for them. When I'm
at church, give me courage to speak Your blessing to the
body of Christ. When I'm alone with a friend, help me
to bless with difficult words if they are needed. Above
all, help me to honor You with the blessings I leave with
others. Amen.

SPEAKING WISE WORDS

My mouth will speak words of wisdom;
the meditation of my heart will
give you understanding.
PSALM 49:3

So often, God, I pray for wisdom in my finances, in my relationships, and in so many other areas of my life. Today, I ask You to simply give me wise words. In every conversation I take part in, give me words of wisdom that encourage and challenge. For every interaction I take part in, give me good, honest, and wise words to speak. And make the thoughts I think today honor You. Prevent me from thinking the wrong things, from saying the wrong things, and from letting my sinful heart rule over me. Amen.

SPEAKING KIND WORDS

*"So then, don't be afraid. I will provide for
you and your children." And he reassured
them and spoke kindly to them.*
Genesis 50:21

Thank You, God, for providing for my family. Thank You
for the food You put on our table, for the money to buy
good things for my family, for my car, my home, and my
things.

I know You provide material blessings, and I don't
have a shortage of things to take care of. I do, however,
struggle with speaking kind words to my family. When my
kids are hurting, I often retreat into my office or garage so
I don't have to engage in their sadness. For those moments, God, give me words of kindness and compassion.
When my wife has had a bad day, I find myself staying
too long at the office, hoping she'll find a way to "unwind"
before I go home. On days like those, give me the courage to instead go home and listen to her and offer her a
kindly listening ear and a word of encouragement.

Lord, give me the courage to be there for my wife
and children—and for others in my circle of family, friends,
and coworkers—when they need me most. And give me
the ability to speak kind words to them. Amen.

3. Wisdom in Serving

LEADING A PRODUCTIVE LIFE

Our people must learn to devote themselves
to doing what is good, in order to provide for
urgent needs and not live unproductive lives.
TITUS 3:14

Thank You, Lord, for the skills and abilities You have given me and for the way You have impassioned me. Thank You also for my time away from work, for the time I have to relax, unwind, and invest in things other than my job.

When I'm not at work, help me to invest in people and in projects that benefit them. Give me focus so that I may clearly see the best places to use the gifts You have given me. Make me a blessing and an encouragement to others in my life—starting with my wife and children.

God, don't allow me to become the kind of man who settles for a life lived from a recliner. Give me boldness and energy to live a productive life for You at all times and in all circumstances. Amen.

LOVE IN ACTION

*Dear children, let us not love with words
or speech but with actions and in truth.*
1 John 3:18

God, I've received many great gifts from people who love me—material gifts and gifts of time and words. These friends have often been Your presence in my life, and they have reminded me of Your reality. Thank You for the gift of these friends.

Now, Lord, help me be an imitator of these dear friends. Help me seek out those who need the gift of my money, time, or words. Lead me by the power of Your Holy Spirit to them, then give me the courage to give. . . food, clothes, money, or anything else they need. And help me to remember that what I give does not belong to me but to You. Thank You for the opportunity to surrender to others what You have given me. Amen.

PUTTING DEEDS BEHIND MY FAITH

But someone will say, "You have faith;
I have deeds." Show me your faith without deeds,
and I will show you my faith by my deeds.
JAMES 2:18

Lord, it is easier to trust in the things I can touch with
my hands and see with my eyes than it is to trust in You.
But I know that isn't how faith in You works. I know You
are preparing things for me that I have not yet seen.

God, please help me trust You and Your promises.
Help me have faith like Abraham, who followed Your
promise for hundreds of miles. Give me the faith of
Moses, who faced down an angry Pharaoh, disbelieving
magicians, and doubting Israelites. Help me to put action
behind my faith and step out and seek to change the
world so that others will have the courage to do what I
am doing.

I love You and thank You for the opportunity to walk
faithfully with You and serve Your kingdom. Amen.

UNDERSTANDING MY DESTINY

For we are God's handiwork, created in Christ Jesus to do good works, which God prepared in advance for us to do.
Ephesians 2:10

God, You created an amazing work of art when You made me. I know there's no one like me on earth, and I know that You have given me unique skills and abilities for the purpose of doing Your will. But I know You didn't create me just so I could hide Your work from the world. So help me put myself out there. Give me courage to show others the good work You have done and are doing in me. Don't allow me to claim any accomplishment as my own—instead, give me the wisdom to return every word of praise I receive back to You, so that others will grasp the power of You working and creating in them, too. Amen.

DEVOTION TO THE COMMANDS OF GOD

You, my brothers and sisters, were called to be free.
But do not use your freedom to indulge the flesh;
rather, serve one another humbly in love.
GALATIANS 5:13

Lord, I know Your laws and commandments because You have clearly revealed them to me in Your written Word, the Bible. But too often I live as though they don't apply to me, as though that they are too old and outdated to make a difference in how I live and serve. So I ignore Your commands and I live by my own rules.

Teach me freedom, Lord, but don't allow me to treat that freedom like a leash that's too long. Help me to grasp Your grace, but don't let me treat it as a license to do whatever I want. I want You to make me into an exact likeness of Christ. I want to love and serve others the way Christ did.

Help me to love Your commands, and help me to live and serve the way Christ did here on earth. And help me become the man You created me to be. Amen.

ENCOURAGING OTHERS TOWARD SERVICE

*And let us consider how we may spur one
another on toward love and good deeds.*
HEBREWS 10:24

Lord, give me words that spur people around me toward
godliness and love for and service to others. Where I see
heartbreak, allow my words to motivate others to provide healing. Where I see brokenness, allow my words
to encourage others to help people toward wholeness.
Where I see poverty, allow my words to motivate others
to give.

Don't let me be the guy who listens to stories of
others' brokenness without offering words of comfort
and wise counsel. Help me to see every person with Your
eyes, and in every situation, act as Your hands by helping
people to become more like Christ as they reach out to
serve and bless others. Amen.

USING GOD'S GIFTS

With this in mind, we constantly pray for you, that our God may make you worthy of his calling, and that by his power he may bring to fruition your every desire for goodness and your every deed prompted by faith.
2 THESSALONIANS 1:11

God, though I have many life goals—ones set by my bosses, by my spouse, and by myself—I know that living according to Your calling for me is the most important task I can accomplish. Help me rise to the challenge of following Your calling on my life.

God, I need Your help to accomplish Your will for me. Too often I doubt my abilities and struggle with self doubt. At times, everything I do seems pointless and ineffective. But I know You equip those You call, so help me see Your giftedness in me and then help me use it to do what You have created me to do. Allow me the pleasure of seeing the effects of Your giftedness in me as I serve others. Amen.

FAITHFUL STEWARDSHIP OF GOD'S GRACE

*Each of you should use whatever gift you have
received to serve others, as faithful stewards
of God's grace in its various forms.*
1 Peter 4:10

Lord, I've received the fullness of Your grace, and it has changed my life. When I was completely lost, Your grace rescued me. When I had nothing, Your grace provided me everything I needed. I have received so much from You, but I still forget to thank You for what You've given me through Your grace; instead I take personal credit for the things I have.

Give me opportunities to give of the grace You've given me. Allow me opportunities to be patient with others, just as You've been patient with me. Allow me opportunities to forgive others, just as You forgive me. Allow me to reach out to others with Your love, just as You reached out to me. Amen.

SERVING WHOLEHEARTEDLY

*Serve wholeheartedly, as if you
were serving the Lord, not people.*
EPHESIANS 6:7

Empty me of myself, Lord, and give me the courage to
sacrifice all of me for Your kingdom and for the good
of those around me. Allow me to never count the cost
of serving others. Give me the passion to surrender all
my time, money, and energy for the good of people
You bring into my life. Help me step into all I do for you
wholeheartedly. Use all of me—my entire body, soul,
and passion—so that others will receive what You have
ordained for them. Thank You for using all of me. Amen.

SERVING THE "LEAST OF THESE"

*"The King will reply, 'Truly I tell you, whatever you
did for one of the least of these brothers
and sisters of mine, you did for me.'"*
Matthew 25:40

God, it's easy for me to judge the homeless and hungry
from behind the window of my car. I've become adept at
coming up with excuses for why I don't need to or can't
help someone who asks for money. I think, *He's an alco-
holic, she does drugs, he's a poor money manager,* or *they
would rather beg for money than work an honest job.*

Jesus, help me to stop thinking up reasons why I
should not help others, and cause me to remember Your
words about how I am to treat the poor. Remind me of
Your command to help others. Don't allow me to see just
a homeless man on a street corner, but rather let me see
You looking for a place to lay Your head. Don't let me be
frustrated that someone is asking for food, but instead
let me see You looking for something to eat. Transform
my understanding of helping others, and allow me the
honor of serving You through giving. Amen.

4. Wisdom for Tough Moments

WHEN MY HOUSE IS BROKEN

*And my God will meet all your needs according
to the riches of his glory in Christ Jesus.*
PHILIPPIANS 4:19

Thank You, Lord, for the house You've given me and
for the things You have put in it. I praise You for my
possessions—for my home, for my car, for my furniture,
and for the other good stuff You have given my family.

Though I work hard, I'm not naive or arrogant
enough to believe that I have obtained anything through
my own labors alone. I know that all I have is a gift from
You, so I ask You to make me a good steward of what
You have given me.

Give me thoughtfulness in how I take care of the
things You have entrusted to me. When we have broken
appliances, give me wisdom as I seek repairs. Help me
to always make the correct decision for maintenance
and repair of my home. Above all, make me a wise
steward who understands that I am only caring for Your
things, not just fixing my broken possessions. Amen.

HEALING MY FRIENDSHIPS

*Even my close friend, someone I trusted,
one who shared my bread, has turned against me.*
PSALM 41:9

God, I lift up to You the disagreement I have had with my close friend. Whatever caused it and however it ended, I am grieving the loss of a friendship. I said the wrong words, and I had the wrong attitude. I'm sorry for how I acted and for what I said.

You have taught that when I'm out of fellowship with a friend, I'm also out of fellowship with You. I don't want to be out of fellowship with him or with You, so please forgive me for the harsh words I spoke, and help me forgive my friend's words. Help me to overcome my own stubborn pride and seek reconciliation with my friend. Give me the strength to seek his forgiveness for my part in the fallout between us.

Thank You, Lord, for the circle of friends You've placed in my life. I value the friendship I've enjoyed with this now-estranged friend, so please repair our relationship and bring us back together. Amen.

THE GOD WHO SEES. . .AND CARES

The LORD is close to the brokenhearted
and saves those who are crushed in spirit.
PSALM 34:18

I love Your broken heart, God. I love that You see everything, including those who are hurting and broken. I love that, despite the fact that You created the entire universe, You can see all the hurt and pain in the entire world. You know about every starving child. You're aware of every broken home. You see every divorce. You know about every empty stomach. Nothing, including the most broken person, escapes Your notice. Thank You for always seeing—and caring. Amen.

RESTORATION, NOT DIVORCE

"The man who hates and divorces his wife," says the Lord, the God of Israel, "does violence to the one he should protect," says the Lord Almighty. So be on your guard, and do not be unfaithful.

MALACHI 2:16

God, I don't always get along with my wife. There are days when we can't agree on anything, days when I imagine myself packing a bag and driving away. While I have never *physically* taken that step, God, I have sometimes *emotionally* divorced her. Sometimes I ignore my wife, and sometimes I treat her like she is my servant. Worse, I envy my friends whose wives *seem* like better spouses than mine. And from there, God, my mind betrays me and leads me into dark places.

God, I need Your help. Please help me to honor my marriage, but more than that, help me to truly love my wife—in my words and in my deeds. Help me to live in peace with her and to respect her. Fill me with the courage to say "I'm sorry" when I do her wrong. Restore my relationship with the woman You've called me to love. Amen.

THE PATH TO HEALING

Is anyone among you sick? Let them call the elders of the church to pray over them and anoint them with oil in the name of the Lord.
JAMES 5:14

Lord, I'm like most men in that it's tough for me to ask others for help. That's especially true when I'm sick. I prefer to suffer alone and struggle through my illness without letting anyone know about it. But after seeing this verse from Your Word, Father, I know that my path to healing runs through asking others to pray for me.

God, I know that You are the Great Physician, and I know that You love healing Your children, so I lift myself up to You and ask You to cover me with Your healing power. And I will also ask others to lift me up and cover me in prayer.

Use doctors, medicines, and even chicken soup to bring healing to my body so that my soul might praise You, my heart might be more fully devoted to You, and others might offer You thanks for my physical healing. Amen.

GOD'S MERCY IN TIMES OF GRIEF

Be merciful to me, Lord, for I am in distress; my eyes grow weak with sorrow, my soul and body with grief.
PSALM 31:9

I've walked through many valleys of grief, Lord. Some days, my sadness is so overwhelming that I don't know if I can go on. My life feels full of broken things—broken relationships, broken bodies, and broken emotions. But I know that You heal *everything*. You fix broken bodies, You heal relationships, and You mend broken hearts. That's what I need You to do now—heal my heart. I need it because I'm covered with grief and sick with heart-ache. Heal my brokenness and fill me with hope. Push me toward healing so I can tell others about the work of my Great Physician. Amen.

PROVISION AFTER A LOST JOB

The Lord is good, a refuge in times of trouble.
He cares for those who trust in him.
NAHUM 1:7

It's hard to believe, God, but after years of hard work, countless hours of time away from my wife and kids, and so much time invested, I've lost my job. I'm bummed, but more than that, I'm hurt. I'm thinking, *Doesn't all the time I've invested in my job mean something? Shouldn't I have the chance to work without fearing that my boss will bring down the hammer for the pettiest things?*

In losing my job, I've also lost my sense of confidence. I don't feel as secure as I once did. And, knowing that my finances are going to suffer, I find myself questioning Your love and provision for me.

I don't want handouts. I want to work and pay my own way. So, God, help me find a good job, one that will allow me to provide for my family, one that will restore my confidence, one that will give me a sense of purpose and identity. I love You and thank You in advance for providing for me. Amen.

FEELING ABANDONED

*Why, L*ord*, do you stand far off?*
Why do you hide yourself in times of trouble?
Psalm 10:1

God, my soul is crying words very much like those of the psalmist: *Where are you, God? Why can't I hear Your voice? Why does it feel like You are so far away from me?*

There are times when You feel as close as my own skin, but in this moment, You feel a million light years away. Despite my attempts to connect with You, right now it feels like there's a brick wall between us. I keep throwing my hands up toward You, but You aren't taking them.

I am waiting for You, Lord. Though my body will move through the day, my soul will be waiting to hear from You. Lord, as I wait, I beg You to honor my waiting by showing up and allowing me to see Your face. Be present, God. Cover me and hold me. Show up and carry me through my day. I need You now. Amen.

HELP FOR TIGHT FINANCES

I was young and now I am old, yet I have never seen the righteous forsaken or their children begging bread.
PSALM 37:25

So many days it seems like there are too many hands in my pockets. No matter how hard I try to save money, my bills are greater than my income. I draw up budgets and try to limit my spending, but nothing seems to work. What's more, it seems that just when my finances are already stretched as tight as they can be, something expensive comes up—car repairs, braces for one of my children. . .the list seems to go on and on.

God, I need help. Help me find creative ways to afford life. Help me tighten my financial belt and make me much wiser in how I spend Your money. Give me wisdom and help me discover ways to cut my expenses. And along the way, Lord, help me to become a giver who blesses those who are more needy than I. Amen.

THE SLAVERY OF DEBT

The rich rule over the poor,
and the borrower is slave to the lender.
PROVERBS 22:7

My eyes long for the things I cannot afford, God. My heart believes that the more toys I have, the happier I'll be. The result of those wayward emotions is this: I've got debt I can't manage, debt that rules over me. You should have the rightful place as the Master over my life, but my financial debt has taken Your place. I should be living free, but my debt weighs me down. I can't travel, can't enjoy myself, can't support missionaries, and can't help hungry people—all because I am too deep in debt.

God, pull me out of this pit. Help me to rely more on You than I do on my credit cards. Give me courage to live within my means. When I need help, help me to be brave enough to ask for it. God, be Lord over my finances, over my family budget, and, most of all, over my debt. Amen.

5. Wisdom in My Relationships

REMOVING BARRIERS TO GOD

Come near to God and he will come near to you.
Wash your hands, you sinners, and purify
your hearts, you double-minded.
JAMES 4:8

God, it's astonishing to know that if I'll simply step toward You, You will step toward me. All I have to do is move into Your presence and You will be there. How amazing. . .the Creator of the universe and the One who knit my DNA together is willing to be with me.

I'm amazed at Your accessibility, God, and I marvel at Your desire to have a relationship with me. But too often my humanity gets in the way of meeting with You, and too often my sin becomes a barrier between us. Help me remove that barrier, God. Give me courage to face and remove the sin that prevents me from being with You. Wash my spiritual hands so that I can hold Yours. Help me discover the way to a pure heart, so mine can be joined with Yours. Amen.

WISDOM FOR MY MARRIAGE

Husbands, in the same way be considerate as you live with your wives, and treat them with respect as the weaker partner and as heirs with you of the gracious gift of life, so that nothing will hinder your prayers.
1 PETER 3:7

God, my wife would never approve of me thinking she's the weaker member of our marriage. She taxis the kids to school and to practices, runs errands, does the shopping, and keeps a fulltime job. Truth is, she works harder than I do. With as hard as she works, I often diminish her accomplishments and treat her as a lesser member of our marriage.

God, help me to love my wife the way You intend me to. Give me the strength to lead her in the way You've commanded me to. Help me love her the way You love me. When I have bad days, don't allow me to take it out on her. Make me a man who loves his wife through all of life's difficulties. Amen.

FINDING CLOSE FRIENDS

Many claim to have unfailing love,
but a faithful person who can find?
PROVERBS 20:6

God, though I know a lot of people, I sometimes don't feel that I have truly close friends—the kind of friends I can truly share myself with, the kind of friends with whom I share mutual love, honesty, and accountability.

I want those kinds of friends, Lord, but more than that, I *need* them. I know that to be the man You created me to be, I need friends who will hold me accountable, who will challenge me to be a better man, and who will encourage me toward godliness.

God, lead me to some truly good friends, ones I can trust and rely upon. Give me friends I can call when I need help handling something I can't do alone. And, God, make me a great friend others can call on for help, rely on, and trust in. Amen.

GODLY PARENTING

Fathers, do not exasperate your children; instead, bring them up in the training and instruction of the Lord.
EPHESIANS 6:4

God, my kids are amazing gifts from You, and I treasure them. They're unique creations, each with their own personalities, gifts, and abilities. Their laughs catch me off guard and fill me with joy. I love watching them as they grow up, interact with one another and with other friends, and do the things they love doing.

I'm grateful for my children, Lord, and I want to show my gratitude for them by being the kind of father You've called me to be. Help me to teach my kids Your Word and help me show them the impact Scripture has had on my life through the way I live and speak in front of them. As I learn more about Christ, help me model His teachings for my kids. Help me control my anger and stress so that nothing gets in the way of my kids seeing exactly who You are. Lead me as I seek to imitate You in every way so that my children can see the reality of Your existence. Amen.

HONORING MY PARENTS

*"Honor your father and your mother, as the
L*ord *your God has commanded you, so that
you may live long and that it may go well with
you in the land the L*ord *your God is giving you."*
Deuteronomy 5:16

I love my parents, God, and I thank You for what they taught me, for the good character traits they passed on to me, and for the way they prepared me for life. I'm grateful for both of them, and I want to be the kind of son who loves his mom and dad in their aging years—both in how I treat them and how I speak to them.

Despite the fact that I've been away from home for so many years, help me to continue to be a good son. Remind me to call or visit just because I want to see them, share my life with them, and invite them to offer their advice. Help me to show my love for them by remembering Father's Day and Mother's Day by calling them or visiting them and by sending cards and gifts.

Thank You for the gift of my parents. Help me show my gratitude by being a gift to them in return. Amen.

RESPECTING MY BOSS

All who are under the yoke of slavery should consider their masters worthy of full respect, so that God's name and our teaching may not be slandered.
1 Timothy 6:1

God, I know that employment is a blessing from You, and I thank You for allowing and enabling me to provide for my family through the work I do. Thank You also for my bosses, those authorities I answer to and who evaluate my performance in the work I've been assigned to do.

Lord, I ask You to bless and protect my employer and my bosses. Give them endurance to do their best as they seek to live up to the expectations of those who oversee them. Help them to have the courage to do the right thing in all situations. Use my words and my performance to encourage them and to further the success and profitability of the company. Help me to be someone who encourages them with kind words and actions. Amen.

HEALING DAMAGED RELATIONSHIPS

Brothers and sisters, do not slander one another. Anyone who speaks against a brother or sister or judges them speaks against the law and judges it. When you judge the law, you are not keeping it, but sitting in judgment on it.
JAMES 4:11

It's so easy to say negative, critical things about people, Lord, and I am often guilty of speaking unkind words. I say negative things about homeless people, those who beg for money, or those who don't look like me or believe the things I believe. As bad as that is, I do the same thing to those closest to me—my friends, my brothers and sisters in church, and even members of my own family. But even worse, I vocalize my harsh words to others, starting a forest fire of negativity that surrounds my friends. My harsh words not only personally hurt those I speak about but also cause others to doubt their character.

Father, forgive me for the critical words I've spoken about those You've called me to love. Give me the courage to confess my wrong and to seek their forgiveness as well as reconciliation and healing. Thank You for being the Healer of relationships—especially those relationships I've damaged with my words. Amen.

LOVING MY SIBLINGS

*Bear with each other and forgive one another
if any of you has a grievance against someone.
Forgive as the Lord forgave you.*
COLOSSIANS 3:13

God, thank You for giving me my siblings. Growing up,
we shared high chairs, blankets, television remotes, and
stories in the back seat of the car. Through the years,
we've grown apart some. We live apart from each other,
and each of us lives busy lives, so we don't talk as much
as we used to. The older we get, the easier it is to forget birthdays and important family events. I miss those
things, Lord. I miss the conversations, the late-night
laughs, the arguments over insignificant things, and
getting into mischief together.

Bless my siblings today, Lord. Encourage them and
strengthen them. Give them peace in their homes. And
remind me today to demonstrate my love for them with
something as simple as a phone call or text—just to
encourage them and let them know I love them. Amen.

BLESSING MY ACQUAINTANCES

*If it is possible, as far as it depends on you,
live at peace with everyone.*
ROMANS 12:18

God, if I were to list the number of people I interact with today, I would need several sheets of paper. Today I'll buy coffee from a busy barista, shake hands with a FedEx driver, tell jokes with the woman in the cubicle next to mine, and do the cool driving wave (two fingers raised on the steering wheel) to countless other drivers.

As I interact with people today, make me a person of love and peace. Help me communicate love to each person I connect with, at whatever level we connect. May Your presence radiate from me and infect others. May Your words come out of my mouth in every conversation. May Your love be evident in every interaction. May Your peace touch each person I connect with today, so that their lives might bring peace to others. Amen.

LOVING MY "ENEMIES"

On the contrary: "If your enemy is hungry, feed him;
if he is thirsty, give him something to drink.
In doing this, you will heap burning coals on his head."
ROMANS 12:20

God, it's so much easier to repay wounds from a "friend" with hurtful, angry actions, and I have a lot of "friends" I feel deserve way more than just my angry words. After the horrible things they've done to me, I feel I have the right to unleash pain on them. Even though Your Word says I should offer food and drink to my enemies, I'd rather let them starve.

I know the way I feel is sinful and wrong, Lord, so please forgive me and help me to live out Your command in Romans 12. Keep me from becoming a man who's known for carrying grudges and seeking revenge. Give me the courage and generosity to seek out those who have hurt me and make those people's lives fuller and better. And never let me forget that I have caused hurt in others' lives, too. Help me to seek forgiveness from those I have harmed, and give them the grace to forgive me, too. Amen.

6. Wisdom for My Finances

WISE SPENDING—AND SAVING

Dishonest money dwindles away, but whoever gathers money little by little makes it grow.
PROVERBS 13:11

Thank You, Lord, for the money You've entrusted to me. I don't take it lightly that You've provided me with *everything* I need—every morsel of food I put into my mouth, every gallon of gas I put in my car, and, maybe more importantly, every dollar I put in my bank account. It's easy for me to lose sight of the fact that everything I have comes from You. But though I work hard for the money I have, I know it is really the result of Your provision.

Help me to be wise with the money You've entrusted to me. Help me to spend wisely on things that will build Your kingdom. Make me a man who invests Your money in his family—his earthly and his eternal family alike—rather than on the latest electronic gadgets, nicest clothes, and newest car. Help me to spend my money the way You'd have me spend it, Lord, and never let me forget that it's wise to save. Amen.

SAVING FOR THE COLLEGE YEARS

*A good person leaves an inheritance for
their children's children, but a sinner's
wealth is stored up for the righteous.*
Proverbs 13:22

This verse is so convicting, Father. When I look at my
finances, I often dream about the cool stuff I could buy
with the money You've provided. I dream of the latest
tablet or a new motor for my boat. I imagine how nice it
would be to upgrade the family car.

While I know it's not necessarily wrong to purchase
those things, I ask You to give me wisdom in handling
what You've given me. Help me have a different mind-set
about my family finances. Make me a man who thinks
ahead and saves money for the future so he can invest
in his kids' education and their life after college. Give me
the supernatural ability to say "no" to all the things I
want right now, and "yes" to saving for tuition, college
textbooks, and meal plans. . .years from now.

Thank You for the gift of being able to use Your money
to provide for my family. Amen.

FREEDOM FROM DEBT

Will not your creditors suddenly arise?
Will they not wake up and make you tremble?
Then you will become their prey.
HABAKKUK 2:7

My desire to have more than I can afford too often gets away from me, God. Where does that desire come from? Why do I want things I cannot afford? Is it because I don't trust You to give me everything I need? Do I worship *things* more than I honor You?

Whatever the reason, I've got debt that I can't repay. I have credit card and student loan debt. I owe for my expensive cars and for my house. And then there are the doctor bills and loans from my friends and my parents.

The amount of money I owe is crippling. When I think about it, I can't breathe and I break into cold sweats. I wonder how I'll manage to repay what I owe while staying on top of my monthly bills, too. God, help me work my way out of this debt. Bring wise people into my life who can help me figure out how pay down my debt. Then help me find a way, by repaying what I owe, to bring glory to Your kingdom. Amen.

WISDOM IN CHOOSING FOOD

*Why spend money on what is not bread, and your labor
on what does not satisfy? Listen, listen to me, and eat
what is good, and you will delight in the richest of fare.*
ISAIAH 55:2

As I look at the areas of my financial life that need Your
touch, God, I recognize that I need to surrender to You
the food I pay for and put in my body. I know that bad
food is bad for my body—and expensive, too. Taking my
family out to eat is almost never as healthy as cooking at
home, and it's nearly always far more costly.

I need help honoring you with food, God. Help me
make wise choices. Help me say "no" to the convenience
(and cost) of eating out too often, and "yes" to preparing
healthy food at home that gives my family better nutri-
tion. Remind me that my body and my finances really
belong to You and that I should honor You in both areas.
Help me and my family to honor our bodies as temples
designed to do the work You've called us to do—and help
me to honor You in my finances by making wise choices
in what and where we eat. Amen.

BLESSINGS IN TITHING

"Bring the whole tithe into the storehouse, that there may be food in my house. Test me in this," says the LORD Almighty, "and see if I will not throw open the floodgates of heaven and pour out so much blessing that there will not be room enough to store it."

MALACHI 3:10

God, Your Word is clear: You call believers to return to You 10 percent of their earnings. In Old Testament times, You intended for the people's tithes to help fund the work of the temple and the priests.

That command—and the reason for it—really hasn't changed, and I know that I must be obedient to it. I know that the wisest thing I can do with Your money is to return it to You, and I know that in order for the church to function the way You want it to, all believers, no matter what economic place they come from, need to surrender Your money back to You in the form of tithes and offerings.

And, of course, I know that You promise a blessing on those who obediently give to Your work here on earth.

But tithing isn't always easy, Lord. In fact, it can be very difficult. I don't always want to open my wallet or write a check. So help me to look past my checkbook balance and obey Your command to tithe. Keep me from allowing fear to control my willingness to give. Thank You for the opportunity You've given me to participate in the funding of Your church—and for the blessings in taking that step. Amen.

GIVING TO THE POOR

If anyone is poor among your fellow Israelites in any of the towns of the land the L<small>ORD</small> your God is giving you, do not be hardhearted or tightfisted toward them.
D<small>EUTERONOMY</small> 15:7

Lord, it feels like I'm a magnet for homeless people everywhere I go. It often seems like I can't stop to put gas in my car or walk into a restaurant without someone approaching me and asking for money. Honestly, God, it can be very annoying—and sometimes a little scary.

But I know Your Word, Lord, and I know this isn't the attitude You want me to have. I know You call me to be a man who has an open hand, who wisely and willingly offers what You've given me to those who need it. Give me opportunities to help others with the money You've put in my bank account. Free me from my fear of the homeless and hungry people who ask me for money, and help me trust You to supply what I need to help them. Amen.

LOANING TO FELLOW CHRISTIANS

"If you lend money to one of my people among you who is needy, do not treat it like a business deal; charge no interest."
EXODUS 22:25

God, I want to be generous to my friends, but I'm struggling financially, too. I don't always have enough money to make it to the end of the month or pay all of my bills. But I want to help my friends, especially my brothers and sisters in You.

Make me a man of faith who willingly lends money to help his friends. Help me to look past my own needs and see the needs of others instead, and then be ready to help with the money they need. And as I surrender Your money to them, change my capitalist heart and help me resist the urge to charge interest. Prevent me from seeking my own gain. Thank You for allowing me to give my friends a hand by helping to pull them out of a financial pinch. Amen.

SAVING FOR RETIREMENT. . .THE RIGHT WAY

Wisdom is a shelter as money is a shelter,
but the advantage of knowledge is this:
Wisdom preserves those who have it.
ECCLESIASTES 7:12

God, I live in a time when every working man and woman is strongly encouraged to prepare for retirement by saving and investing. And while I want to be able to provide for myself and my spouse after I leave the world of work, I'm not completely sure how I should accomplish that goal. Should I work myself into submission—at the expense of spending time with my family. . .and of my own sanity?

That just doesn't seem wise to me. I want a good life, and I want to enjoy my family. I want those things for my entire life. . .now and in the future, including those years after I retire. For now, as I work and save for retirement, help me to remember to savor every moment You give me with my family and friends. At the same time, give me the wisdom I need to prepare for those retirement years. Amen.

KINDNESS TO THE POOR

*Whoever is kind to the poor lends to the L*ORD*,*
and he will reward them for what they have done.
PROVERBS 19:17

Lord, it's easy for me to ignore the hungry people in my community. I see them as they stand at traffic signals and drive-through lines holding signs, but I don't really *see* them. In some ways, I don't really regard them as *real* people.

God, open my eyes to these people. Make them real to me. Don't allow their hunger to be invisible to me, and don't allow me to ignore their needs. And, while I love being rewarded for helping others, don't let my desire for compensation overshadow my pure passion to help others. Make me Your servant and use me to reach the invisible people. . .the ones who remain invisible to most of us. Amen.

RADICAL SURRENDER

Jesus looked at him and loved him. "One thing you lack," he said. "Go, sell everything you have and give to the poor, and you will have treasure in heaven. Then come, follow me."
MARK 10:21

Jesus, your words here are hard. . .*too* hard. How can I sell *everything* I have and then give it all away to the poor? Do You really expect me to live in poverty just so others can have food, clothing, and shelter? Or are Your words figurative, like in other parts of the Bible, and You expect me to have an attitude of radical surrender?

I know I can trust You and that You intend every word You spoke to teach me what it means to be like You. So help me live out the words You spoke to the rich young ruler. Help me develop an attitude of surrender. Help me to see things in my life that I can do without, and help me surrender them to You. And God, help me and guide me as I apply Your words to my life. Amen.

7. Wisdom in My Workplace

CLEAR-MINDEDNESS AT WORK

But you, keep your head in all situations,
endure hardship, do the work of an evangelist,
discharge all the duties of your ministry.
2 TIMOTHY 4:5

Jesus, I know that productivity begins with good organization. As I look at my coworkers' cubicles and offices, I see how they keep files arranged, how their desks look, and how well they're organized. I'm envious of their filing and their workstations—at least some of them.

Teach me to organize like they do—to have a workspace that suits me and a desk that screams organization. Don't allow messiness to take over. Don't allow my tendency to rush from task to task to ruin my organization and create piles of uncompleted tasks that litter my workspace. Help me to think about where I work and about how I organize myself. And help me to impress my coworkers with the way I manage my office. Thank You for my job, Father. Amen.

RESPECT FOR AUTHORITY

Have confidence in your leaders and submit to their authority, because they keep watch over you as those who must give an account. Do this so that their work will be a joy, not a burden, for that would be of no benefit to you.
HEBREWS 13:17

I love my job, Lord. I love where I work, and I love my coworkers. When I walk into my workplace each morning, I think about how fortunate I am to have a job I love.

But my workplace isn't quite heaven on earth. Though I get along well with everyone, there are times when it's not easy to respect my coworkers or my boss. Sometimes I feel like my boss expects way too much from me but has lower expectations of others.

Lord, in those moments when my boss starts pushing my buttons, help me to respond to him with the respect due him because of his place over me. Give me the grace to work for him just as I'd work for You—with the very best effort I can muster. Help me to love and respect those I work with—my boss as well as my coworkers— at all times, no matter what. Amen.

THE SOURCE OF ENDURANCE

We remember before our God and Father your work produced by faith, your labor prompted by love, and your endurance inspired by hope in our Lord Jesus Christ.
1 THESSALONIANS 1:3

While I love my job, there are days—sometimes several in a row—when I just want to stay home. I feel tired and empty, and I miss time with my friends and family. In those times, it feels like work comes around too often. I get home, fall asleep on the couch, wake up after the kids are asleep, crawl into my bed, get up the next morning—and then repeat that over again.

If I could ask You for anything during times like these, Father, it would be endurance. I need Your energy to fill me so that I can be amazing at work. I need Your energy in me so that I can live a full life. Fill me with endurance so that I can do the work You've given me to do. Amen.

HONESTY IN ALL THINGS

For we are taking pains to do what is right, not only in the eyes of the Lord but also in the eyes of man.
2 Corinthians 8:21

Honesty these days is a rare treasure, God. People cheat on their taxes, cheat at work, cheat on family and friends. Why is dishonesty so easy and so prevalent? Is it because lying is one of the few sins we can do in secret? So many of us choose not to tell the truth, believing that others won't discover our little secret.

But You see everything, God. You know when we're telling the truth, and You see us when we're lying.

It's easy for me to easily slide down into the liar's pit—at work and other places. Help me to tell the truth in every circumstance. Help me to be a man who speaks what is right and true to every person I meet and in every situation I encounter. Amen.

TAMING THE TONGUE

The tongue also is a fire, a world of evil among the parts of the body. It corrupts the whole body, sets the whole course of one's life on fire, and is itself set on fire by hell.

JAMES 3:6

Lord, I'm good—very, *very* good—at hurting others with the words I speak. I unleash my tongue on everyone—sometimes in anger, sometimes under my breath. Sometimes I'm arrogantly mean to people's faces. It doesn't matter where I am, to whom I'm speaking, or when I say it. . .I use my tongue to hurt others. And gossip is often my good friend—especially at work.

Lord, help me to stop this. Prevent me from saying things that should not be said and from hurting others with my words. I need You to help me keep my mouth shut, especially when I have the opportunity to unleash anger, lies, and secrets about people I work with. Instead, help me to speak only good things about my boss and my coworkers. Bless and guide every word that comes out of my mouth. Amen.

GOD'S LOVE IN TIMES OF BUSYNESS

*I press on toward the goal to win the prize for which
God has called me heavenward in Christ Jesus.*
PHILIPPIANS 3:14

When I'm buried under work, Lord, I know You're there.
When I've got people breathing down my neck, waiting
for whatever project I'm committed to, I know You're
there, too. You're present in the ickiness, in the stress, in
the loneliness of feeling stranded in the middle of assign-
ments and to-do lists.

But tasks often scream louder than Your love, Father.
Though I know You're always present, I often cannot feel
You with me. Help me remain diligent to what I have to
do, so that I don't have to feel buried. Narrow my focus
and set my eyes on the important things. Be present
with me in these difficult moments, and help me to feel
Your love. Amen.

GRACE FOR MY COWORKERS

As God's co-workers we urge you not to receive God's grace in vain. For he says, "In the time of my favor I heard you, and in the day of salvation I helped you." I tell you, now is the time of God's favor, now is the day of salvation.
2 CORINTHIANS 6:1–2

God, I'm very good at watching everyone else work, and I've perfected the art of criticizing others' performances. When secretaries stand around talking for most of the day, I quickly cast stones. When my boss spends hours on the internet, I imagine myself telling him off. When my peers waste time doing the most inane tasks, I get angry.

There are days when I feel like I'm the only one working. I know that when I feel like I'm working harder than others, what I'm feeling is a partly righteous anger. But I also know that I'm judging others, and I know You don't want me to do that.

Help me to treat my coworkers with love and grace. Help me turn from judging and to focus more on my own work. I know it's important for me to work peaceably with others, so help me do that—especially on the days when I struggle with my attitudes toward my coworkers. Amen.

FINDING SATISFACTION IN MY WORK

For he satisfies the thirsty,
and fills the hungry with good things.
Psalm 107:9

Lord, so often I begin a new week by mumbling a depressed "Here we go again. . ." Truth is, my life seems mundane at times. Every week consists of the same boring list of tasks I need to accomplish. At times, I feel like my life consists only of work, work, and more work. I need satisfaction in what I do for a living. I also need excitement, adventure, and fun.

God, help me find something amazing and exciting in life to lean into. And help me do more than just get up and go to work every day of every week. Help me create a sense of adventure where I work, and empower me to help my coworkers find satisfaction as well. Amen.

DILIGENCE IN MY WORK

Whatever you do, work at it with all your heart,
as working for the Lord, not for human masters.
COLOSSIANS 3:23

I pursue a lot of things, God—career, hobbies, adventures with my family. I know I invest in the things that interest me with great passion, so help me to invest myself in my work as passionately as I invest myself in my other interests. Give me endurance so I can stay on-task at work. I need clear focus to complete the tasks I've been given, and I ask You to give me that focus by reminding me daily that I'm working for You, not just for the company that employs me. Thank You for giving me my job and for challenging me and giving me an opportunity to honor You with the work I do. Amen.

WORK HOURS ARE FOR WORK

A sluggard's appetite is never filled,
but the desires of the diligent are fully satisfied.
PROVERBS 13:4

God, I don't want to be "that guy" at work—the one who's known for living off the hard work of others. I don't want to be the one who sits around drinking coffee while others work hard to meet company deadlines.

I know that a sluggard—a none-too-flattering word for a lazy person—is always hungry, and I know that You've called me to work hard for my employer, my family, and my future. So give me focus in the workplace. Help me to stay diligent to what You have given me to do. Above all, God, help me work hard so that my desires will be satisfied. Amen.

8. Wisdom in My Spiritual Life

PASSION FOR PRAYER AND THE WORD OF GOD

The Sovereign Lord has given me a well-instructed tongue, to know the word that sustains the weary. He wakens me morning by morning, wakens my ear to listen like one being instructed.

ISAIAH 50:4

God, I know I need to be more consistent with my prayer life, and I know I need to study Your Word more consistently, too. I know that nothing can feed my soul more than your thoughts. But God, it's so hard to make time to talk to You and read the Bible. And I'll confess that sometimes I just don't feel very interested in doing either.

But I want to *want* to pray and read the Bible. So please give me that desire. Fill me with a passion for prayer and for Your Word. Make me thirst for silence, hymns, and stillness that only come from rich prayer to You. Cause me to surrender myself in prayer, seeking only Your face and Your presence. And give me a supernatural understanding of what You tell me in Scripture. Make me a man whose passion is to be in Your presence. I am waiting now for You. Fill me with all of who You are. Amen.

BIBLE STORIES

*For everything that was written in the past was
written to teach us, so that through the endurance
taught in the Scriptures and the encouragement
they provide we might have hope.*
ROMANS 15:4

God, I know that everything in Your Word is true, right,
and correct. I know that You've inspired men to write the
Bible to provide me the wisdom and instruction I need to
live faithfully for You.

I love the stories You've recorded in Scripture. Those
stories have helped shape my understanding of You and
my relationship with You.

I'm thankful for the times we have together when I
read Your Word and pray to You. I know that the Bible
has everything I need for my life with You. Continue to
lead me back to Your Word and to use it to cleanse my
heart. Help me to apply the lessons from the stories in
Your Word in my own life. Amen.

DEVOTED TO DEVOTION

Devote yourselves to prayer,
being watchful and thankful.
COLOSSIANS 4:2

Devoted is such an important word, God. I know it's important that I be devoted to You in all things. There's a stillness that comes with devotion to You—as well as a mind
that easily turns to prayer and a soul that effortlessly
slips into watchfulness.

I know the biblical stories of the people of devotion.
They're my heroes, God, and I aspire to be like them.
Lord, make me like those men in Your Word who always
had their eyes set on You. Make my walk like their walk,
my commitment like their commitment.

I know that my inner life is important, God. I know
that silence in Your presence is filling, and that talking
to You is essential. I know that time spent reading Your
Word is more important that time spent in the gym. So,
make me watchful. Make me devoted. Make me a man of
Your Word, a man quick to study, a man quick to turn to
You. Amen.

FINDING SILENT MOMENTS

Tremble and do not sin; when you are on your beds,
search your hearts and be silent.
PSALM 4:4

There's so much noise in my life, God. My cell phone constantly draws me away from what's important, and my job always seems to encroach on my family time and my time with You. If I'm not careful, my responsibilities can draw me away from You. But I know that time with You is essential and the only way I'll grow as a believer.

Lord, help me to be silent and find moments when I can be still and listen for Your voice. Help me find places where I won't be interrupted, where I can focus only on You. Silence my phone for me when I don't have the courage to silence it myself. Help me ignore my e-mail when I just can't find it within myself to turn off my computer. In every area of my life, make the silence of Your presence louder than the interruptions. Amen.

MY GOD IS ENOUGH

*I say to myself, "The Lord is my portion;
therefore I will wait for him."*
LAMENTATIONS 3:24

God, help me to know that You are all I need. Teach me that I don't *need* a newer car or more money in my bank account. Teach me that I don't need anything in addition to You. When I'm with my friends, help me to not be envious of their possessions, and remind me that jealousy is unhealthy. Help me to trust You and to delight in who You are and what You are, and cause me to be satisfied with everything You give me. Thank You for being everything I need. Amen.

WORSHIPPING BY HEARING THE WORD

Until I come, devote yourself to the public reading of Scripture, to preaching and to teaching.
1 TIMOTHY 4:13

God, I love looking at Your face. I count myself fortunate to have opportunities to stand with other believers in Your presence. I love joining with other believers and worshipping You with singing. And when I worship, I love hearing the proclamation of Your Word.

As I seek out worship experiences with You, make me a man who is devoted to Your Word, a man who is willing to read Your Word in public, a man who is eager to hear Your Word preached. And make me sensitive to Your Spirit, so that I am able to do the things Your Word challenges me to do. Amen.

LIVING BY FAITH

*For in the gospel the righteousness of God is revealed—
a righteousness that is by faith from first to last,
just as it is written: "The righteous will live by faith."*
ROMANS 1:17

God, I know that You love righteous people. But the truth is that I don't feel like a righteous man. I don't see the faith in my life that I see in the men I read about in the Bible. I don't have David's ability to trust You for everything, Peter's ability to live boldly for You, or Paul's ability to speak the truth in every situation.

I know that living by faith is the one ingredient I need to be considered Your kind of man. So God, please give me that faith. Help me to trust You with everything I have and for everything I need. Give me the courage to live the kind of righteous life I see in the lives of the people in Scripture. Amen.

POWER IN FASTING

*It will not be obvious to others that you are fasting,
but only to your Father, who is unseen; and your Father,
who sees what is done in secret, will reward you.*
MATTHEW 6:18

Lord, Your Word tells me that fasting can be a power-ful companion to my prayers to You. But there are few things in my life more difficult than surrendering food. You know how much I love to eat. You know that to me, sitting down to a good hamburger is like sitting down at the door of heaven.

It's not that I don't love You, only that I've grown accustomed to having the food I want when I want it. To me, food isn't always about fueling my body but also about the tastes, smells, and satisfaction eating brings to me. I hate admitting it, but food is a god to me. I don't build altars to tacos or pray to hamburgers, but my soul definitely bows at the altar of fast food.

Make me strong enough to surrender my eating to You. Help me remove my worship of food so that I can worship only You. Convince me that I need to surrender, if only for a short time, the food I crave, so that I can crave You on a deeper level. Amen.

SEEKING GOD'S CLEANSING

*Let us draw near to God with a sincere heart and with
the full assurance that faith brings, having our hearts
sprinkled to cleanse us from a guilty conscience and
having our bodies washed with pure water.*
HEBREWS 10:22

I'm dirty, God, and I need Your cleansing. My soul is
covered with the mud of sin, and the world has darkened
my spirit. My desire to be good and righteous has waned,
and I look more like the world than I look like You.

But I know that You long to see me whole and clean
and to have me back in Your presence. God, make me
open to Your cleansing. Help me to want Your Holy Spirit.
Create in me a desire to have Your Spirit cleanse me,
despite the pain and discomfort that cleansing might
cause. I know that Your presence in me is the only path to
living holy. So do what You have to do. Cleanse me, mold
me, and shape me—and do it all so that I can be a new
creation, holy and ready to serve You. Amen.

CONFESSION OF SIN

If we confess our sins, he is faithful and just and will forgive us our sins and purify us from all unrighteousness.
1 JOHN 1:9

It's too easy to be strong, God, and with strength comes the desire to always be right. Please save me from my need to always be right. Save me from my inability to surrender my will. Most of all, help me overcome my desire to ignore my sin.

Lord, You know I'm very good at blaming others or my situations for my sinful actions and thoughts—and very bad at admitting when I'm wrong. I know salvation is found only in You, and that it only comes when I confess what I've done wrong. Help me to say I'm sorry and to ask for Your cleansing and forgiveness. And when I ask You to forgive me, fill me with the knowledge that You love me and have washed me clean. Amen.

9. Wisdom in Battling Temptation

ANGER WITHOUT SIN

*"In your anger do not sin": Do not let
the sun go down while you are still angry.*
EPHESIANS 4:26

Lord, it's a rare moment when I don't feel some kind of anger. Sometimes it's anger over what's going on at work. I also get angry in traffic when other drivers frustrate me. At times, I'm short-tempered with my kids when they push my buttons. And I've also gotten angry when my neighbors are too loud.

Lord, help me learn the difference between anger that motivates me toward righteousness and anger that causes me to sin. It's too easy for me to sin, and sin badly, when I'm angry. So remove from me the temptation to lose my temper, and fill me with peace. Teach me how to control my anger so that it doesn't get the best of me. And help me be honest when I am angry with someone, and give me the courage and wisdom to sp~~~~ in a more loving, gentler way. Amen.

AVOIDING "WORKAHOLISM"

*There was a man all alone; he had neither son nor brother.
There was no end to his toil, yet his eyes were not
content with his wealth. "For whom am I toiling," he
asked, "and why am I depriving myself of enjoyment?"
This too is meaningless—a miserable business!*
ECCLESIASTES 4:8

Lord, I know it's not possible to gain the whole world, but
it often feels like I'm trying to do just that. I know You
encourage people to work hard, but I think I really overdo
it at times. *How do people have time for a life and work?*
I wonder. *Is it possible to actually have fun, spend time
with my family and friends, and just relax?* When I look
at the time I invest in everything I've said ye to at work,
I'm not so sure it is.

God, help me to leave work at work and find time to
invest in myself and in my family and friends. Give me
a sense of healthy boundaries. Help me know when I'm
working too much and keeping an unhealthy schedule.
Help me to listen to people who love me and honor their
encouragement to leave work at work. I know you have
an amazing adventure waiting for me, so don't let me live
entire life in my cubicle—and miss out because of it.

CONTROLLING MY THOUGHT LIFE

Put to death, therefore, whatever belongs to your earthly nature: sexual immorality, impurity, lust, evil desires and greed, which is idolatry.
COLOSSIANS 3:5

I'm thankful for the way you made me, God, but I sometimes wonder if You didn't add a little too much testosterone to the mix. I say that because I often struggle with looking at women and entertaining what I know are impure thoughts. I know those thoughts don't honor You, Lord, and I have to confess that there are times when all of me wants to go where my mind has already gone.

I know this is not Your will for me, Lord. I know You want to help me control my thoughts better than I have. I ask you to help me keep my mind from wandering into sinful places. Help me to see women as Your creations, as valuable people with a purpose and an eternal soul. Keep my mind from using others sexually and from objectifying women. Help me to flee from this sin, so that I may honor You as I honor others. Amen.

LOVE FOR MY FAMILY

Only be careful, and watch yourselves closely so that you do not forget the things your eyes have seen or let them fade from your heart as long as you live. Teach them to your children and to their children after them.
DEUTERONOMY 4:9

This is my simple prayer, Lord: help me to love my family. Help me to overcome the temptation to minimize them, in my words and actions alike. Help me to live life *with* them, not separate *from* them. Help me say "no" to additional work commitments and "yes" to fun, quality time with my wife and children. When I am with them, help me to speak kind and loving words—words that create for them a positive environment at home. When I am with my children, help me to love them by giving them all my attention. Help me to model for my sons what being a godly man looks like, and help me to demonstrate for my daughters how a husband treats his wife. Give me the presence of mind to recall Scripture when I'm with them. I want to be my kids' biggest hero and their favorite teacher of Your truth. Amen.

GOD'S GENEROUS GIFTS

*But remember the Lord your God, for it is he who gives
you the ability to produce wealth, and so confirms his
covenant, which he swore to your ancestors, as it is today.*
DEUTERONOMY 8:18

Lord, I marvel at the unique abilities You give each and
every person. When I look within my own family, I'm in
awe of their giftedness, which shows itself in their ability
to provide for their own families.

Lord, You have made me just as uniquely gifted as
those around me. Sometimes, however, I lose sight of the
fact that my own talents and gifts come straight from You.

When I forget that it is You who gives me the ability
to produce an income, I am tempted to become careless
with the money You have provided. Please help me to
stop thinking of the income You provide me as *my* money
and start thinking of it as *Yours*. Give me the wisdom to
recognize when I am spending frivolously on things my
family and I don't really need. Let me be generous with
You, Lord, and with those You direct my way. Thank You
for Your generosity. Amen.

A RIGHTEOUS ESCAPE

*No temptation has overtaken you except what
is common to mankind. And God is faithful;
he will not let you be tempted beyond what
you can bear. But when you are tempted, he will
also provide a way out so that you can endure it.*
1 CORINTHIANS 10:13

There have been times, Lord, when I've been tempted to
leave all of my responsibilities behind and escape to an
island somewhere. . .permanently. Life can be so heavy,
and the pressure on me is overwhelming at times. There
are weeks, sometimes months, at a time when I feel like
I am drowning, and leaving it all behind seems like the
best alternative.

I do take comfort in knowing that this is a common
temptation. That may be why there are so many broken
homes—men feel the pressures of life, and they believe
their only escape is just to walk away from everything.

But I don't want that to be me, Lord. You are a faithful God, and when my faith is weak and my flesh doesn't
want to be faithful, please be faithful for both of us. Show
me the righteous way out of this temptation to escape,
Lord, so that I can endure life when it seems so overwhelming. Thank You for listening to me, and thank You
for being my only real escape. Amen.

WORSHIPPING GOD ALONE

"You shall have no other gods before me."
EXODUS 20:3

God, You existed before there was anything. Before the world existed, You formed molecules, atoms, matter, and then DNA. You created light and darkness, the planets, and vegetation. You are the creator of all life. Humanity walked on earth because You lovingly breathed life into Adam and Eve. Cities exist, communities flourish, and nations thrive because of Your loving kindness. You are all-powerful, all-knowing, all-loving, and all-kind.

Help me to worship only You, my great Creator, because only You are worthy. Help me to avoid the temptation to put anything ahead of you. Give me strength to keep my eyes on You only and to worship You with all that I am. Amen.

KEEPING FOOD AND DRINK IN THEIR PLACE

*Do not join those who drink too much
wine or gorge themselves on meat.*
PROVERBS 23:20

It's easy to medicate stress with substances these days, God. When work gets too hard and stress becomes too great, eating and drinking too much are quite a temptation. I know that Your Word warns me against eating and drinking too much and against allowing anything—including food and drink—to become a god to me.

Forgive me for those moments when I have indulged in excessive food or drink instead of handing my stress over to You. In all things and in every area of my life, help me to rely on You only. Keep me from using anything as a crutch or a bandage. Thank You, God, that I can lean on You. Amen.

ACHIEVING SUCCESS GOD'S WAY

*Those who want to get rich fall into temptation and a
trap and into many foolish and harmful desires
that plunge people into ruin and destruction.*
1 TIMOTHY 6:9

Make me a builder, Lord—someone who builds up others,
who seeks to make people better than they are presently.
Help me avoid the temptation of letting my desire for
wealth or power impede my ability to serve. Create in me
a passion to make others successful.

Don't allow me to build financial success at the
expense of personal relationships. Keep me from filling
my checkbook while emptying myself of all ethics and
morality. As I seek to build wealth, help me to avoid
temptations to lie and cheat.

I don't want to get rich at the expense of others, so as
I seek to build savings to provide for family and friends,
help me to place love alongside hard work. Help me to
put serving next to sacrifice. Thank You in advance for
rescuing me from any of those temptations and for moti-
vating me to achieve financial success Your way. Amen.

BEING A GODLY LEADER

When I was a child, I talked like a child, I thought like a child, I reasoned like a child. When I became a man, I put the ways of childhood behind me.
1 Corinthians 13:11

Lord, it is so easy for me to treat my family like my servants. I am tempted to let my wife do all the cooking and cleaning. Or to come home from work and bark out my kids' names and demand that they quiet down as I plop down in my recliner. Lord, I now clearly see that this is childish thinking. So help me to man up and love my family by being the leader of my family that You have called me to be.

Lord, it doesn't stop there. I have refused my responsibilities as a leader within my church. Help me to put childish ways behind me and be a true godly leader within my faith community.

Jesus, I am humbled when I think of the heavenly splendor You left for me—and for the example You set of sacrificial leadership. And I am also motivated to be the kind of leader You were here on earth. Help me, Lord, to live a life of sacrifice for others—just like You did. Amen.

10. Wisdom about the Kingdom of God and Heaven

HOPE FOR AN ETERNAL HOME

*But in keeping with his promise we are
looking forward to a new heaven and a
new earth, where righteousness dwells.*
2 PETER 3:13

It's easy, God, to lose sight of where You want me to go and to choose my own way. Even though Your Word tells me that I'm called to be a kingdom person—a person who lives life with an eye toward eternity—I often opt for the temporary.

Your call for me to shift my focus away from earthly things is so much better for me. It's a call to hope in heaven, a call to wait for Your coming. I know that if I am patient and faithful, You will give me an eternal home with You.

God, I want to dwell eternally in Your presence, in Your righteousness, and in Your kingdom. Help me to patiently wait for that moment when I can open my eyes in heaven. Until then, make me a man who loves You more than he loves this temporary earth. Thank You for making a place for me. Amen.

BEARING GOOD FRUIT. . .FOR THE RIGHT REASON

But the wisdom that comes from heaven is first of all pure; then peace-loving, considerate, submissive, full of mercy and good fruit, impartial and sincere.
JAMES 3:17

God, I confess that nearly every good thing I do is for the purpose of building my own kingdom. I offer to help my next-door neighbor because I know I'll need his help in the future. I give money and tell people I'm giving so that they'll look favorably on me. I show up at all the right parties, events, and service opportunities because I know that being in those places makes me look good.

My selfishness is building a kingdom in which every person who is watching glorifies *me*. But You have taught me how wrong and backward that approach really is. Help me to do my good works with a sincere heart toward helping others and advancing Your kingdom. I don't want to be a Christian who honors You with my mouth but not with my true intent. Make me selfless, sincere, and wise in all I do and say. My desire is that You know me as a man who passionately pursues Your kingdom—and passionately pursues being like You. Amen.

WAITING FOR HEAVEN

For while we are in this tent, we groan and are burdened, because we do not wish to be unclothed but to be clothed instead with our heavenly dwelling, so that what is mortal may be swallowed up by life.
2 Corinthians 5:4

Lord, I'm ready to be with You in heaven. I'm ready to kneel at Your feet, wrap my arms around Your ankles, and just be in Your presence. I'm ready to listen to the sounds of heaven—the voices of the saints singing Your praises. I'm ready to leave every worldly stress I live with, every problem I face, and every tough issue I deal with. I know that where You dwell, everything is perfect, and I'm ready to live with You in perfect eternity.

But I know I have a mission for me here on earth while I wait. I know You've created me to do good works for You. So help me to be patient while I wait. And while I'm waiting, help me to see the places and situations in which I can use the gifts You've given me to help others feel the excitement about that moment when they open their eyes for the first time in Your presence. Amen.

BEING TEACHABLE

"Therefore anyone who sets aside one of the least of these commands and teaches others accordingly will be called least in the kingdom of heaven, but whoever practices and teaches these commands will be called great in the kingdom of heaven."
MATTHEW 5:19

Father, there's such a huge gulf between hearing and doing. So many men I know are adept at hearing Your Word. They've perfected the art of investing time studying the Bible, and many of them are known for the amount of scripture they can recall and teach to others. But there's a difference between being a teacher and being teachable.

Lord, please make me a teachable man. Make my soul ready to hear what You have to say and to live by what I hear. Give me the courage to put into practice the truth You've revealed in Your written Word. Wherever I'm living and whatever I'm doing, help me to boldly proclaim You through everything I say, everything I do, and everything I am. Amen.

CHILDLIKE FAITH

"Truly I tell you, anyone who will not receive the kingdom of God like a little child will never enter it."
MARK 10:15

Lord, I confess that being an adult has caused me to complicate my relationship with You. I've taken the simplest concepts of faith, hope, and love, and I've created little to-do lists for each one. I've lost the wonder and excitement I once had for my relationship with You.

I want that childlike faith again, but work, broken things around my house, family budgets, and everything else that comes with being a grownup gets in the way. I want to see Your kingdom and to be with You for eternity. Help me to embrace eternity like a child—with simple trust. Help me to trust who You are and Your promises.

When I need a reminder of how to live by this kind of faith, bring to mind my own children and other children I know, and help me learn from the way they live. Thank You for what You taught about the blessings of childlike faith in You. Amen.

TRUE KINGDOM FAITH

"Woe to you, teachers of the law and Pharisees, you hypocrites! You shut the door of the kingdom of heaven in people's faces. You yourselves do not enter, nor will you let those enter who are trying to."
<small>MATTHEW 23:13</small>

Lord Jesus, too many churches today seem to do a great job of keeping people out of Your kingdom. Please don't let me be a man who does the same thing. Don't allow my passion for You to dissolve into a meaningless system of religious practices. Don't allow me to take Your sacrifice on the Cross for granted. Don't let me think that my accomplishments are my own doing. And don't allow me to think that I have better access to You than others do.

I know that when You walked the earth, you spoke harshly against those who relied on religious practices and laws. I don't want to be one of those guys, either. Keep me from being a person who makes living for You a difficult series of rules. Give me perspective, and help me remember where I will spend eternity. While I am still physically alive, help me to live like a kingdom person—in a way that makes me ready to enter Your kingdom. Amen.

SEEKING KNOWLEDGE

He said, "The knowledge of the secrets of the kingdom of God has been given to you, but to others I speak in parables, so that, " 'though seeing, they may not see; though hearing, they may not understand.' "
LUKE 8:10

God, I'm glad that Your knowledge is way beyond the earthly kind, and I'm glad that Your thoughts transcend the physical universe I live in right now.

Things on earth are so temporary and finite, and humanity's knowledge and wisdom aren't just limited but also flawed. The worldly places I can turn for knowledge and wisdom are just as flawed. The wisdom of my peers—flawed. The wisdom of leaders around me—flawed. The wisdom of pastors, even the well-intentioned ones—flawed. But Your knowledge and wisdom are amazing simply because they are infinite—and perfect. Give me Your perfect wisdom, God, and I'll be able to live the life that honors You in everything I do. Amen.

BEING BORN AGAIN

*Jesus answered, "Very truly I tell you,
no one can enter the kingdom of God
unless they are born of water and the Spirit."*
JOHN 3:5

Jesus, thank You for saving me, for giving new life to my soul, and for teaching me a new way to live. When I think of my old way of living and thinking, I'm more keenly aware of the gift You've given me. My eternal destination has changed, so I no longer have to fear death. My present has changed, so now my focus is not on myself but on pleasing You. And You've also revolutionized my understanding of joy.

I know that this gift is only possible because You willingly died on the cross for me. Now I look forward to entering eternity with You. Until then, give me the courage to tell others about this incredible gift, and cause me to live with gratitude for the work You've done in me. Amen.

ENDURING HARDSHIP

Strengthening the disciples and encouraging them to remain true to the faith. "We must go through many hardships to enter the kingdom of God," they said.
Acts 14:22

Lord, like most men, I hate hardships. To be honest, I have difficulty understanding how hard times can help prepare me to enter Your kingdom. It seems like life in You should be easier than that. But I trust Your Word and believe what You say.

So God, please give me the endurance I need to live this life. Help me to set my eyes not on the temporary things—like my job and my possessions—but on eternity in heaven. Lord, make life with You in heaven for all eternity my goal. Give me the courage and the focus I need to live every day, even the most difficult ones, with that in mind. Amen.

PERSONAL RIGHTEOUSNESS

*For the kingdom of God is not a matter of
eating and drinking, but of righteousness,
peace and joy in the Holy Spirit.*
ROMANS 14:17

I'm a Pharisee in a lot of ways, God. I spend my time
worrying about the righteousness of other men. I see the
way they spend their money, and I judge them. I listen to
the way they talk to their wives, and I criticize them.

It doesn't take much for me to pull Scripture out of
my head to use to judge others. But I struggle to apply
Your words in Romans 14 to my own life. That's why it's
so much easier for me to focus my effort on outward
spirituality than inward.

I know that's not how You operate, God, and I'm
aware that if I'm going to be Your child, I've got to work
on my own soul first. So, help me discover a righteousness that isn't dependent on others' spirituality. Help me
to craft a personal walk that focuses only on You and
the way You lived. Do this so that I can be the man You
created me to be. Amen.

11. Wisdom on the Fruit of the Spirit

LIVING IN THE LOVE OF GOD

No one has ever seen God; but if we love one another,
God lives in us and his love is made complete in us.
1 JOHN 4:12

I love the way You love me, God. I love hearing Your encouraging words, and I love it when I feel Your presence. I know You are not physically with me, but I know You're present in my life because I love those in the community of faith, and they love me in return.

So, Lord, when I see others who need Your love, help me to love them the way You love me. Give me courage to offer a loving embrace or encouraging words. Help me to put on display the fruit of Your Holy Spirit called love. And, finally, remind me that the love I offer others is proof positive that You live in me. Amen.

FILLED WITH HOPE AND JOY

*May the God of hope fill you with all joy and peace
as you trust in him, so that you may overflow
with hope by the power of the Holy Spirit.*
Romans 15:13

Lord, Your Word promises that You will fill me with hope and joy. I'm a man who is desperate for joy and who needs hope in his life right now. So today I ask You for both.

I want to be someone who is known for his attitude of hopefulness and joy, even in the most difficult situations. So today I pray in faith, asking that You fill me with both hope and joy. Remind me daily that my hope is in You and in the promise of eternal life with You in heaven. And help me to remember that my joy is also to be in You, not in any external circumstances. God, I pray that through the power of Your Spirit, You will cause me to overflow with hope and joy to the point that others will see it and be affected by it as well. In Your holy name, Amen.

LIVING IN PEACE

Finally, brothers and sisters, rejoice! Strive for full restoration, encourage one another, be of one mind, live in peace. And the God of love and peace will be with you.
2 Corinthians 13:11

God, You are the Author and Creator of all good things. Thank You for creating peace. When I am overwhelmed and stressed, I know I can rely on Your presence to calm me. Help me every day to tap into Your quieting Spirit and to rely on Your presence. When I have discord with others, help me bring peace into the situation. In moments when those close to me are feeling stressed, give me words that will bring them inner peace. Above all, let my own soul enjoy the peace You've promised those who love You and live for You. Amen.

THE BLESSINGS OF PATIENCE

*And we urge you, brothers and sisters, warn those
who are idle and disruptive, encourage the disheartened,
help the weak, be patient with everyone.*
1 THESSALONIANS 5:14

God, technology has led our world to a place where we
humans expect everything to happen at the speed of a
mouse click. Everything in life happens so quickly—we
demand instant answers, next-day delivery, and fast food.
I'll admit that I've been well-trained as a person who no
longer needs to be patient about anything.

But I know You don't see time the way I do, Lord. I
know You very often wait to work things out according
to Your perfect will and at the perfect time. So teach
me to be patient and wait on You. And don't let me rush
through important moments. Instead, give me the ability
to savor every memory You are creating. Help me learn
patience so I don't miss a moment with my family, with
my kids, with my friends, or with You. Amen.

CLOTHED IN KINDNESS

*Therefore, as God's chosen people, holy and
dearly loved, clothe yourselves with compassion,
kindness, humility, gentleness and patience.*
Colossians 3:12

Lord, I admit that I'm a man with some rough edges.
I can be testy, and I'm often quick to anger. I struggle
with the need to be in control. And when I'm in control,
I tend to manipulate events so that things go my way.
My need to be in charge has led me to become a man
who too often lacks humility and kindness. In Your love,
remove these rough edges. Soothe my need to control
every situation and make every difficult decision. Fill me
with kindness and compassion and replace my will with
Yours so that I will be known as a man who is truly
clothed in kindness. Amen.

ADDING GOODNESS

For this very reason, make every effort to add to your faith goodness; and to goodness, knowledge.
2 PETER 1:5

Jesus, I am so many things—a husband, a father, an employee, a son—and I wear many hats and have many responsibilities. But in my pursuit of success in the work world, I have made some bad decisions. Specifically, I have chosen myself and my work over my family, friends, and coworkers. Where I should have sought the good of others, I sought good only for myself.

Lord, You came to earth to be the Servant of many, but I've served no one but myself. My desire to be seen as successful has led me to neglect and forget others. God, I want You to make me good—and not just good but filled with *godly* goodness. Make me a good man so that I can take advantage of every opportunity to help others see *Your* goodness. Amen.

MODELING FAITHFULNESS

*It gave me great joy when some believers came
and testified about your faithfulness to the truth,
telling how you continue to walk in it.*
3 John 1:3

Lord, I need people in my life I can follow. Help me to find men of faith who have fought the good fight, sought You through every circumstance, and have demonstrated the value of faithfulness to You in how they lived. Help me to find men whose lives I can rejoice in, who can be my examples for how to live a life in You. And make these men role models who can help me be a man whose faith others testify about. Thank You for the honor of living a life that seeks to model You and influence others for Your kingdom. Amen.

A LIFE MARKED BY SELF-CONTROL

Teach the older men to be temperate,
worthy of respect, self-controlled,
and sound in faith, in love and in endurance.
TITUS 2:2

Lord, Your words in Titus 2 offer me an amazing list of character traits to want You to instill in me. Father, please make me temperate and slow to anger. Make me truly worthy of the respect of everyone who knows me. Make my actions those worthy of a Christ follower. And fill me with self-control in every area of my life.

God, I ask You to help me to show self-control in all my dealings and in all my relationships—with my neighbors, my friends, my enemies, my coworkers, and my family. Fill me with Your love so that it flows out of me without limits. As I grow in my relationship with You, make my life one that is marked by godly, consistent self-control. Amen.

THE SPIRIT OF SONSHIP

Because you are his sons, God sent the Spirit of his Son into our hearts, the Spirit who calls out, "Abba, Father."
GALATIANS 4:6

Lord, today I commit to thinking of You always as my spiritual Father. Just as an earthly child relies on his father for nourishment, I choose to rely on You for every morsel of food I put in my mouth. I will rely on You for every decision at my job. I will invite You into every decision for parenting my kids, and I will bring my wife to You, and together we will seek You for the future of our family. Like a son busting with pride for his dad, I will show my neighbors the love I have for You. I will honor You with every act of my will and emotion. Thank You for loving me as Your son. Help me to love You fully as my Dad. Amen.

GOD'S DWELLING PLACE

And in him you too are being built together to
become a dwelling in which God lives by his Spirit.
EPHESIANS 2:22

Thanks, God, for knitting me together with my friends
and family. I love the community You've surrounded me
with, and I love my church family. I love that You've surrounded me with my personal heroes of the faith, people I can trust and can follow. But what I love the most,
God, is that as I live with these people, work with them,
worship with them, and serve beside them, You are there,
present with all of us. You don't just band us together
and then leave us on our own; You stand with us when
we are together. Thank You for making us into a dwelling
place so that You can live among us. Amen.

12. Wisdom from the Prophets

REMEMBERING THE SOURCE

*L<small>ORD</small>, you establish peace for us; all that we
have accomplished you have done for us.*
I<small>SAIAH</small> 26:12

Pride is a killer, God, and I have to confess that I struggle
with it. I have perfected the art of aiming the spotlight on
myself and taking credit for my accomplishments.

Though I am sometimes quick to take the credit, I am
not ignorant of where my success comes from. So, Jesus,
help me stop and praise You each day for what You are
using me to accomplish. And then help me to show others Your strength in me so that they can understand that
though I am doing the work, it's really You working in and
through me. Amen.

KEEPING MY VOWS

*"But I, with shouts of grateful praise, will sacrifice
to you. What I have vowed I will make good.
I will say, 'Salvation comes from the LORD.'"*
JONAH 2:9

Lord, when I read the Bible, I can clearly see that You're a
promise keeper. When You promise prosperity, You give
it. When You promise judgment, You deliver it. I cannot make the kind of promises You make. I cannot heal
someone's leg or forgive someone's sins. But I can be a
man who keeps his word. I can be a father who keeps his
promise to be a good father by investing his time and
other resources in his kids. I can be a man who loves his
wife—which I vowed to do when I married. So, help me
be a man who keeps his word no matter how much difficulty or sacrifice is required. Amen.

WHAT GOD REALLY DESIRES

For I desire mercy, not sacrifice, and acknowledgment of God rather than burnt offerings.
HOSEA 6:6

Lord, a lot of my life has been guided by this truth: Your thoughts are not my thoughts. I fully acknowledge that I'll never be able to understand Your thinking, God. I know that the things You do are often best explained as mysteries. But there are some things about You I don't have to wonder about. I know that You require mercy from me and that You want me to be a man who always defers to others. And I know that You'd rather have me live in Your grace than worry about following every tiny rule in Your Word.

Lord, give me the words to help others understand Your character. Help me explain the power of living under grace. Make me a man who understands the law but who also understands the freedom of living under the shadow of Your grace. Amen.

THE SOURCE OF WISDOM

*For you created my inmost being; you knit
me together in my mother's womb. I praise you
because I am fearfully and wonderfully made;
your works are wonderful, I know that full well.*
Isaiah 139:13-14

God, You knew me before I was being formed in my mother's womb. You saw my face and knew me before anyone else. As You formed me, You built skill and passion within me, preparing me to do Your work here on the earth.

As I grow and pursue what You've created me to be and do, please give me Your wisdom. Help me to know the correct path to take and the correct way to live. Help me to know how to best spend my money and invest my time. Do whatever You must to make me the man You intended me to be—even before You formed me in my mother's womb. Amen.

ASKING FOR RESTORATION

Restore us to yourself, L\ord, that we may return;
renew our days as of old.
LAMENTATIONS 5:21

Lord, I felt so close to You when we first met. You were my closest friend, and I used to talk to You about everything, big and small. Then, little by little, life crept in.

I'm thankful for my family and for the work You've given me to do. But somehow in the bustle of life of caring for my family and working, You have taken a back seat in my life. There are days I don't talk to You or even think about You. And on the days when I try to pray, it often seems forced and contrived.

I'm sorry, Lord, for letting so many things come between us. Please forgive me. I miss You, and I want the relationship we had at the beginning. Help me to set aside the time needed to restore the closeness I once enjoyed with You. Amen.

YIELDING TO GOD'S DIRECTION

LORD, I know that people's lives are not their own;
it is not for them to direct their steps.
JEREMIAH 10:23

Lord, I like to be in control, and that's because it feels safe to me. When I can be in charge of my environment, emotions, and plans, then the future doesn't seem to be such an unknown.

I know how to manage my life pretty well. . .most of the time. But that changes when I, or someone I love, goes through a crisis, like getting sick or losing a job. And I will admit that when life gets hard, I can become very angry with You, Lord—because I wanted to be in control.

Father, sometimes the direction You choose for me seems difficult. But help me to remember that You love me and want the best for me. Keep me yielded to Your control and direction for my life. I love You, Lord, for Your patience with me. Amen.

FEARING THE LORD

*But be sure to fear the Lord and serve him faithfully
with all your heart; consider what great
things he has done for you.*
1 Samuel 12:24

Lord, I stand in awe of the amazing things You have done
for my family. You provided housing when we were in
need. You have given me good friends and a wonderful
family.

God, if You can do all these things for me, then I
know on a personal level that You are a God to be wor-
shipped and respected. Lord, You have my heart, and
I will serve You faithfully all my life. Thank You for the
great things You have done for me. Amen.

TRUSTING THE LORD

"Don't be afraid," the prophet answered. "Those who are with us are more than those who are with them."
2 Kings 6:16

God, it is so easy to see what is in front of me and feel intimidated. I'm trying so hard to do well all the work You've given my hands to do, but sometimes it seems like the harder I try, the more difficult the task becomes. I then feel frustrated, so I try harder. Then the resistance seems to multiply and I get discouraged.

Lord, remind me in those moments that what I face is not a physical battle, but a spiritual one. Open my eyes of discernment so that I can see what is really taking place in the spiritual realm. Help me not to become discouraged when I feel attacked, but rather trust that You will sort all things out. Thank You for being with me, Lord. Amen.

ASKING GOD TO REVEAL HIMSELF

"Answer me, Lord, answer me, so these people will know that you, Lord, are God, and that you are turning their hearts back again."
1 Kings 18:37

Lord, it has been such a long time since I've heard Your voice, and I need to hear from You. I've been crying out to You for an answer, but I've heard nothing but silence. In the past, I heard from You all the time. I would talk to You and You would speak to me. I would hear Your voice in books, through art, in song, and through Your written Word. But now, it's all silence, and I feel like I am in a desert begging for water that's too long in coming.

My friends aren't helpful, either. Some don't believe in You and wonder why I still ask You to answer me. Others are sure that I've brought Your silence upon myself, that I must have done something wrong and refuse to repent.

Please answer me, not just for my sake, but also for the sake of those who are watching to see what You will do. Amen.

PUTTING GOD'S WORD INTO PRACTICE

*"My people come to you, as they usually do,
and sit before you to hear your words, but they
do not put them into practice. Their mouths speak
of love, but their hearts are greedy for unjust gain."*
EZEKIEL 33:31

Week after week, I sit in the pew at church and listen to the words You've given my pastor to speak. Week after week, I leave my seat, shake my pastor's hand, and tell him what a great message he gave. But you know the truth, Lord. You know it's all just an act. I don't mind critiquing his oration or research methods. But if what he's preached on is too difficult or makes me feel uncomfortable, there is no way I'm going to do it.

I'm very good at finding spiritual-sounding excuses for why I don't need to do what You've asked of me. Lord, forgive me. Soften my heart and give me the courage to be obedient. Help me to love You with more than just my words. Amen.

13. Wisdom from Old Testament Heroes

MOSES—STANDING ON HOLY GROUND

*"Do not come any closer," God said.
"Take off your sandals, for the place
where you are standing is holy ground."*
Exodus 3:5

Cause me to be observant, Lord. Let me start each day intentionally looking for holy places—places where You are dwelling. Give me eyes to see Your flame burning and ears to hear Your voice calling. Keep me from being so distracted by the routine of life that I miss You right in front of me. And when I have found the holy place You have called me to, help me to live in that moment. I want to take off my shoes like Moses did, and I want to recognize that You are present there with me. I pray that in that moment I would trust You and not be afraid. Amen.

ABRAHAM—A FRIEND OF GOD

*Our God, did you not drive out the inhabitants
of this land before your people Israel and give it
forever to the descendants of Abraham your friend?*
2 Chronicles 20:7

God, there's so much about Your character woven throughout the Old Testament. When I read about how You led the Israelites out of Egyptian captivity, I'm most impressed by Your saving character. When I read about how You loved the people of Israel even through their spiritual adultery, I'm amazed at Your faithfulness.

In Your sovereignty, You prepared the land You had chosen for Israel to inhabit. No one loves to that extent or is filled with that much grace. I am astonished that in the midst of Your holiness and my sinfulness, You chose to call me Your friend. Help me to live my life in such a way that when others see me, they see our friendship. Amen.

JOSEPH—A MAN OF INTEGRITY

"No one is greater in this house than I am.
My master has withheld nothing from me except you,
because you are his wife. How then could I do
such a wicked thing and sin against God?"
GENESIS 39:9

I want to be a man of integrity, God. I have so much to be thankful for, and I don't want to do anything to ruin it. And besides, doing the right thing is important to me. I want to finish the task You've given me, even when it's difficult.

Lord, keep my feet from straying from the path You have set for me. Busy my hands with the job You've assigned me. Hold my heart close to Yours so I can know what real love is. Set my eyes on You so I won't sin against You. Amen.

JOSHUA—COURAGE PERSONIFIED

"Have I not commanded you? Be strong and courageous. Do not be afraid; do not be discouraged, for the LORD your God will be with you wherever you go."
JOSHUA 1:9

God, I try not to look too far into the future, mostly because I'm often paralyzed with fear at what You have asked of me. So grant me the courage to accomplish seemingly insurmountable tasks.

I often don't feel like I have what it takes to do the job You've set before me. Every instinct within me cries out for me to run. I know that someone else can do what You've asked better than I can, and I wonder why You asked me. And I fear that I will I fail and bring shame on You, myself and my family. Then what will I do and say?

Lord, I'm riddled with fear and self-doubt. Help me to see what You see in me. Silence the voices of fear and doubt that constantly whisper in my ear. Keep reminding me that You are with me wherever I go. Show me that You are my ever-present God, who loves and cares for me. Thank You, Lord. Amen.

DAVID—A MAN AFTER GOD'S OWN HEART

"After removing Saul, he made David their king.
God testified concerning him: 'I have found David
son of Jesse, a man after my own heart; he will
do everything I want him to do.' "
ACTS 13:22

Will I do everything You ask of me, Lord? I want to, but You and I both know I'm weak. I know I'll make mistakes. I'm easily distracted by pretty, shiny things. I chase after things I shouldn't, things I know aren't intended for me.

When I stumble and fall, help me to remain open to Your discipline. Keep my heart tender. I don't want to make excuses for my sin, and I don't want to blame You for choosing a path of disobedience. I want to be a man after Your own heart so that I can be the person You have created me to be. I love You, and I want to honor You with my life. Amen.

SOLOMON—WISDOM ON DISPLAY

*The whole world sought audience with Solomon
to hear the wisdom God had put in his heart.*
1 KINGS 10:24

God, I feel a bit like Solomon right now. "The whole
world" wants me to have answers for them. My boss and
coworkers want answers. My wife and kids and friends
want answers. Creditors want answers.

The difference between Solomon and me, though,
is that I don't feel very wise. I feel exhausted. I feel like
I need a break from the world so I can just sit in silence
for a week or two. Since that is unlikely, Lord, my guess is
that people will continue to seek me out.

Please help me to know what to say to each person
who contacts me. Help me to be an encouragement,
and grant me the courage to speak truth in love when the
need arises. Give me the insight to see the real need and
solution. Lord, remind me that wisdom comes from You.
Thank You, God, for Your desire to share Your wisdom
with me—if I only ask for it. Amen.

NOAH—UNCOMMON RIGHTEOUSNESS

This is the account of Noah and his family. Noah was a righteous man, blameless among the people of his time, and he walked faithfully with God.
GENESIS 6:9

Lord, I try to live my life in such a way that no one can accuse me of wrongdoing. When I stand before You, I want to be blameless and hear You say, "Well done!"

But have I walked faithfully with You? Do I do all of the "right" things because it's in my nature to do them and because it brings me satisfaction? Or am I faithfully walking with You, knowing that my righteousness is from You alone and brings You glory? Lord, I want to be a man who walks faithfully with You. Keep drawing me back to You when I wander. Thank You for Your faithfulness to me. Amen.

SAMUEL—LISTENING TO GOD

The Lord came and stood there, calling as at the other times, "Samuel! Samuel!" Then Samuel said, "Speak, for your servant is listening."
1 SAMUEL 3:10

How many times will You have to call to me, Lord, before I recognize Your voice? Teach me to shut out the noise of the world around me and be attentive to You only. Remind me to seek the quiet and stillness and just listen for You. In those moments when I am unsure if the voice I am hearing is Yours or someone else's, provide a wise guide for me to turn to.

Lord, I long to hear Your voice—but just as it was in Samuel's day, it seems that You don't speak very often. Or is it that You do speak and I'm just not listening? God, give me the listening ears of Samuel and the willing heart to do what I hear You telling me to do. Keep me close to Your heart as You whisper Your words of love and instruction in my ear. Speak, for Your servant is listening. Amen.

JACOB—WRESTLING WITH GOD

*Then the man said, "Your name will no longer be
Jacob, but Israel, because you have struggled
with God and with humans and have overcome."*
GENESIS 32:28

I have wrestled with You my whole life, Lord. You were
my parents' God, my pastor's God, and my wife's God.
I have a rich history of church attendance and service.
I've been taught and discipled by some amazing men who
know You and Your Word well. I feel that I've been following after You my whole life, and yet I feel like something is missing. I have all of this knowledge *about* You,
but I wonder sometimes if I really know You personally. It
seems that You've always been someone else's God.

Lord, please be *my* God. Give me peace as I overcome
my fear and doubt and surrender myself to You without
reservation. Amen.

EZRA—STUDYING GOD'S WORD

*For Ezra had devoted himself to the study
and observance of the Law of the L*ord*,
and to teaching its decrees and laws in Israel.*
Ezra 7:10

Thank You, Lord, for Your written Word. There are so many treasures within the pages of Scripture for me to find. Each time I devote myself to studying Your Word, You are faithful to show me something new. I am amazed at the beauty and intricacy of the story of Your love for humanity.

I know You want me to put personal effort into reading and studying Your Word. But it's so easy to allow others to do my reading and studying for me, Lord. Please don't let me become lazy. Help me shed my preconceived ideas about Your Word and study it myself in the way You intended. Thank You for revealing Your love for me through Your Word. Amen.

14. Wisdom from Jesus

DENYING MYSELF

*Then Jesus said to his disciples, "Whoever wants
to be my disciple must deny themselves and
take up their cross and follow me."*
MATTHEW 16:24

Jesus, it's so hard to deny myself the things I want. . .and
so easy to rationalize why I should have them. That bag of
chips, the bottle of soda, the big-screen television—they
all call to me. After all, I work hard day after day, and I
need to unwind. And why should I deny myself any of
these things in the first place?

Lord, help me to remember that life's existence is
about more than mere pleasure. Thank You for setting
the example of that truth for me by leaving the treasures
of heaven and denying Yourself—all for higher purpose.
Christ, I want to be so unattached to the things of this life
that I don't think twice about denying any or all of them
for Your sake. Help me to keep my eyes on the treasures
of heaven rather than the pleasures of earth. Amen.

CLOSE AT HAND

*Jesus looked at them and said, "With man this
is impossible, but with God all things are possible."*
Matthew 19:26

I don't see a way out, Lord. I've tried everything I know to
do, but this mountain in front of me still seems impossible
to climb. My friends ridicule me. In their eyes, I am weak
because I am unable to accomplish the task before me.

But You, Lord, dwell in the impossible spaces. It is
there that You love to show Your glory. Reach out to
me, God. Take my frustration, fear, and humiliation and
turn them into a shining testimony that You are the God
of the impossible. Jesus, remind me always that when
things seem impossible, You are close at hand. Thank You
for that promise. Amen.

THE GREAT PHYSICIAN

On hearing this, Jesus said to them, "It is not the healthy who need a doctor, but the sick. I have not come to call the righteous, but sinners."
MARK 2:17

Jesus, show me those places of sickness in me. Reveal the areas of sinfulness in my life. I don't like having those things pointed out to me, Lord. I like to think that I am living my life right and that I'm not a "bad" person. But if my own righteousness keeps You from coming near me, strip it away and show me where I need Your healing touch.

I want to be healthy so I can follow You wherever You lead. Give me Your righteousness, Lord, and continue to be my Great Physician when the hurts in this life become more than I can bear. Thank You for being willing to get Your hands dirty with my crud. Amen.

A CHOSEN MESSENGER

*Jesus did not let him, but said, "Go home to your
own people and tell them how much the Lord has
done for you, and how he has had mercy on you."*
MARK 5:19

Lord, You have done so much for me, but I sometimes
forget the goodness and mercy You have shown me in
abundance. You have given me everything I could ever
want or need, and yet I neglect to speak words of gratitude and praise.

Though I am sometimes slow to say it, I am grateful
to You and humbled that You would take the time to
care for my needs. I ask that You use my gratefulness to
embolden me to talk to others, even those I don't know,
about what You have done for me. Bring the right people
across my path for me to tell about Your love and care.
Prepare their hearts to hear about You. Most of all, Lord,
keep me sensitive to Your voice. Thank You, Jesus, for
doing so much for me. And thank You for choosing me to
be a messenger of Your grace and mercy. Amen.

GIVING AND FOLLOWING

*Jesus answered, "If you want to be perfect, go,
sell your possessions and give to the poor, and you
will have treasure in heaven. Then come, follow me."*
MATTHEW 19:21

Jesus, giving away my money is hard for me to do. I don't
mind giving away my time, talent, or advice, but I cringe
when You ask me to give my money. I am a good father
and husband, and I work hard to provide for my family.
I am a leader in my church, and I even serve the poor in
my community and periodically go on mission trips. Isn't
that enough?

God, You know I've wrestled with this issue ever
since we met—and You know I have many excuses for
why I can't give. I know You love me, and I know You
understand the struggle going on inside me. Continue to
patiently work on me. Help me to love and trust You so
much that I no longer fear giving my money. Amen.

THE POWER TO HEAL

But Jesus said, "Someone touched me;
I know that power has gone out from me."
LUKE 8:46

Jesus, I'm hurting. I've looked for help in many places, but the pain is still here. I just can't seem to shake it. It has affected the way I relate to those around me. In many ways, I feel ostracized and left out, and that only adds to my pain, Lord.

I know You are a God who has the power to heal. Would You heal me? Is it possible to get close enough to touch You? I don't want a faith healer, Jesus—I want You. I want to know that I've come close enough to You that You feel and see Your healing power go out from You. Let me come that near to You. Please touch the hurt and heal me. Amen.

THE GREAT PROVIDER

*Then Jesus said to his disciples: "Therefore I
tell you, do not worry about your life, what you
will eat; or about your body, what you will wear."*
LUKE 12:22

Lord, You have placed within me the desire to provide
for my family. I want to give them good things, but those
things—college education, braces, glasses, cars, and
insurance—come at a price. I try not to be concerned or
worried, but the bills keep coming. How can I *not* give
good things to my family, and yet how can I afford it?
Lord, it seems that no matter how much or how little I
make, I worry. I'm afraid that my worry is going to kill me
someday.

Lord, help me to trust that You love my family more
than I do—and that You will provide everything we need.
Bring to my mind all the times You have faithfully provided
for us in the past, so that the voices telling me it will all fall
apart are silenced. Thank You that I don't have to do life
on my own. Thank You that I have a heavenly Father who
is always there and never runs out of resources. Amen.

A HEALING FAITH

Jesus said to him, "Receive your sight;
your faith has healed you."
LUKE 18:42

I'm struggling, Jesus. I know You are the God who heals.
I've seen You do it in my life and in others' lives before.
But now this illness is causing me to crack. My faith is as
strong now as it was then. So what's the difference? Why
haven't You chosen to heal me this time?

Some people around me tell me that if I just had a
little more faith, You would listen and heal. Is that true,
Lord? If so, then I'm begging for You to listen to me and
heal me. Either way, my faith is in You, Jesus. I know that
You can heal me, and I am asking that You will. But if
You choose to bring more glory to Yourself through this
illness, please keep my faith in You strong. Be my friend
and close companion through all of it. Amen.

GOD AT WORK

In his defense Jesus said to them,
"My Father is always at
his work to this very day,
and I too am working."
JOHN 5:17

It is so encouraging to know that You are always at work in this world, Lord. When I look around me and see the chaos of the world—wars, financial instability, hunger, illness, moral decay, corruption—it can be easy for me to wonder if You have forgotten about us. I live in a world that has walked away from You, and it feels like You have walked away from us in return.

Jesus, help me to see Your work in the middle of the chaos. As the storm of life rages around me, keep my eyes on You. Show me Your work of seeking and saving the lost. Lord, if You can use me, I am willing. Amen.

A REFRESHING SPRING

*On the last and greatest day of the festival, Jesus stood
and said in a loud voice, "Let anyone
who is thirsty come to me and drink."*
JOHN 7:37

Jesus, You are a refreshing spring of water on a hot summer's day. When my tongue is swollen and my throat is dry, I draw long mouthfuls of cool water past my cracked lips. I can feel the cold radiating down my throat, refreshing every fiber of my body. My fingertips and toes are tingling with the sensation of that drink.

Lord, when I drink in Your Word, sing about You, and worship You, my dry spirit is refreshed. Lord, keep me coming to You. Please don't let me get bored or curious and then try to substitute other things for what You alone have to give: life-sustaining drink. Amen.

15. Wisdom from the Sermon on the Mount

POOR IN SPIRIT

*"Blessed are the poor in spirit,
for theirs is the kingdom of heaven."*
Matthew 5:3

Forgive me, Lord, for believing I need to always be strong. So often, I want to be the one others can rely on. I want to be the first guy called on when there's a tragedy. But I know that the way into Your kingdom isn't through unbridled strength, but through sometimes allowing myself to be weak.

God, forgive me also for believing I always have to be happy, upbeat, and positive. Help me honor and worship You when I am feeling sad—when I am "poor in spirit"—and in those moments when I am going through a valley, please remind me that You are preparing me for a life lived in Your kingdom. Amen.

COMFORT IN TIMES OF MOURNING

*"Blessed are those who mourn,
for they will be comforted."*
MATTHEW 5:4

Lord, there are days when I'm overwhelmed with sadness. Work is hard, ends don't meet, and I'm in disagreement with everyone. In those times, life overwhelms me, sadness takes root, and I mourn. But as real as those emotions are, I know that true mourning is much deeper, that it is rooted in critical life experiences. As dark as my life can get, I know that others around me are dealing with even deeper pain.

God, I pray that You would meet, comfort, and heal those around me who are mourning the loss of friends, children, relationships, jobs, and anything else that has been taken from them. Wash over them and fill them with relief and grace. Don't allow them to suffer in silence, but make me aware of their wall of grief and motivate me to be Your hands and feet. Amen.

A MEEK SPIRIT

"Blessed are the meek,
for they will inherit the earth."
MATTHEW 5:5

The world tells me that I deserve so many things, God—a nicer house, a bigger car, more money, credit cards. I'm told all the time that in order to be a successful man, I need to be the best at my job and that happiness comes as the result of hard work and connectedness.

But Your Word says something different. The Bible tells me that success, prosperity, and financial blessings all come as the result of meekness and that blessings come from surrendering my will for Yours. Blessings come not from humiliating myself, but from humbling myself—not from allowing others to step all over me, but from allowing others to have first place.

So, God, give me a meek spirit. Allow me to let others win so that I may gain through You. Allow me the opportunity to inherit whatever You want me to, but only through leaving myself behind and wholly following You. Amen.

CRAVING RIGHTEOUSNESS

*"Blessed are those who hunger and thirst
for righteousness, for they will be filled."*
MATTHEW 5:6

God, I know that Your righteousness is the only thing I need, that it is better than anything I could ever dream of possessing. I long for financial success, but Your righteousness is better than all the riches in the world. I wonder what it would be like to be famous, but I know that Your righteousness is far better than being known throughout the world.

The more I read Your Word, the more I understand that righteousness is simply the passion to be like You, to know Your Word, and to passionately live like Christ. Please give me the ability to do all those things. Make me hungrier for righteousness than I am for food, for a warm house to sleep in, for clean clothes to wear, or for life itself. And, God, know that I am waiting on the fulfillment of Your promise to fill me with the righteousness I long for. Amen.

MERCIFUL LIVING

"Blessed are the merciful,
for they will be shown mercy."
MATTHEW 5:7

It's not in my nature to let up, God. I prefer to push hard at people, at accomplishments, and for more possessions. Because of my desire to have more and to be more, I often walk on and over others and make them feel less than who You created them to be. To put it bluntly, I struggle with showing mercy.

It's just too easy for me to be in charge. I'm a good quarterback in every situation—at work and at home. Lord, forgive me for always needing to take control and for trying to push people around. Fill me with so much mercy that it spills out of me in every circumstance. Fill me with godliness, holiness, and goodness. Amen.

PURITY OF HEART

*"Blessed are the pure in heart,
for they will see God."*
MATTHEW 5:8

Jesus, Your Word tells me that no one has ever seen You face to face. But it also tells me that some of my favorite Bible heroes caught a glimpse of Your glory. I have to admit that thinking of seeing Your glory like that makes me feel a little envious. But that feeling fades away when I think of Your promise that the pure in heart will one day get to see God Himself.

Lord, make my heart open to allowing You to do whatever it takes to purify me to the point where I can one day stare at Your face and can revel in Your presence and study Your holiness up close. Allow me to live in the purity You call me to, and give me a passion to be like You in how I live, how I think, and how I treat others. Make me a man who is so connected to you that others will know me as one who lives with a passion for Your purity and holiness. Amen.

BEING A PEACEMAKER

*"Blessed are the peacemakers,
for they will be called children of God."*
MATTHEW 5:9

Lord, so many of my close friends seem to live in a constant state of conflict. They argue with their kids, with their parents, and with their spouses. I know there's no peace in these men's homes. And while I'm on the subject, I must confess that there's no peace in my home, either.

God, make me a peacemaker in my home. Help me to avoid arguments with my wife, and keep me from being the kind of father who exasperates and frustrates his children with constant nit-picking. Guide me in my conversations with my spouse and my kids, and keep me from being the guy whose words tear down his family instead of building them up. Make me a man who seeks peace and reconciliation, even in the most difficult circumstances. Amen.

PERSECUTED FOR RIGHTEOUSNESS

"Blessed are those who are persecuted because of righteousness, for theirs is the kingdom of heaven."
MATTHEW 5:10

God, though I've never been overtly persecuted for loving You, I have wondered if I wasn't promoted at work because others know that I go to church. I have suspected that my parents, though I'm a grown man, still belittle my beliefs as "immature." And many times, I have felt like those close to me have secretly made fun of me because I trust and love You.

Your Word promises that Your kingdom will be mine—*because* of those times when I am ignored, ridiculed, or mocked for my faith in You. When I feel persecuted, remind me of Your promise. Help me remember my future as a kingdom dweller. Remind me of Your love for me and Your protection over me. Thank You for Your loving protection. Amen.

SALT OF THE EARTH

*"You are the salt of the earth. But if the salt
loses its saltiness, how can it be made salty
again? It is no longer good for anything,
except to be thrown out and trampled underfoot."*
MATTHEW 5:13

Thanks for putting me in the world, God. Thanks for allowing me to experience everything that the world has to offer—good food and fun experiences like boating, running, swimming, and so many other things.

As I live my amazing life, help me to be a godly influence on those around me. Give me the opportunity to tell others about You, about Your mercy and grace. Give me opportunities to serve others who are less fortunate. Help me to speak about the changes You've made in my life and the good things You've made happen in my family. Help me be "salty" as I direct others' attention toward You. Thank You for opportunities to help others see You more clearly. Amen.

SHINING LIGHT

"In the same way, let your light shine before others, that they may see your good deeds and glorify your Father in heaven."
MATTHEW 5:16

God, I confess that I'm a light-hider. I'm better at telling gross jokes than I am at telling others about You. When I'm in a room darkened by sin, I'm quicker to participate in darkness than I am to help others understand the light inside me.

Lord, Your call to me is clear. You want me to raise the standard, to be the person who helps others see truth and goodness and who shows others that there's a better way to live. You want me to help others understand the difference between sin and holiness. So help me steer clear of darkness. But more than that, give me the courage to shine the light of Your love in dark places. Help me to shine Your light on everyone I'm around, no matter where I am, no matter how evil the surroundings. Make me a man who lives a holy life, so others can clearly see You. Amen.

16. Wisdom from the Wise (Proverbs)

WISDOM WITH FRIENDSHIPS

Wounds from a friend can be trusted,
but an enemy multiplies kisses.
PROVERBS 27:6

Lord, the more time I spend in my workplace, the more difficult it becomes to know the difference between a friend and an enemy. Those who seemed to be in my corner suddenly seem to be working against me. And some days the meanest coworker comes through as my biggest ally.

God, give me the patience I need to deal with friends who sometimes seem like enemies. Help me offer grace to those who have issues with my decisions and my actions. Help me rely on Your sovereignty, and keep me from lashing out at those who seem like enemies. Above all, Lord, help me to live at peace with others around me, and give me the grace to reply to every harsh word or action with Your love. Amen.

AVOIDING PERVERSE WORDS

Keep your mouth free of perversity;
keep corrupt talk far from your lips.
PROVERBS 4:24

Lord, I know it's important to be a man who speaks honestly, who speaks clearly, and who doesn't invest his words in hurting others. I know that Your Word commands me to stay way away from words, phrases, and ideas that harm others.

I ask that You keep my mouth from perverse talk. Remind me of the damage coarse talk does to other men. Remind me that it doesn't honor You when I tell dirty jokes, use inappropriate words, or slander others. Before I open my mouth, remind me of my commitments to my family, my friends, and, most importantly, to You. Help me keep my speech in check, and cause me to only say things that honor You. Amen.

PRAISE FROM OTHERS

*Let someone else praise you, and not your own
mouth; an outsider, and not your own lips.*
PROVERBS 27:2

God, surround me with good friends, with people who
see the good in me, who take notice of the ways I strive
to be like You in every area of my life. And also help me
to remain humble.

It's easy for me to praise myself to my friends and
in public, and I confess that I do that a lot. I'm good at
talking about my skills and talents and accomplishments.
Help me keep my mouth shut, God, and help me sit back
and allow others to speak good things about me—if they
so choose. Tighten my lips, and loosen others'. Keep
me from praising myself and remind me often to speak
words of praise to You. Amen.

DON'T BE A BRAGGART

*Do not boast about tomorrow, for you
do not know what a day may bring.*
PROVERBS 27:1

God, I confess that I'd rather talk about my accomplishments than just about anything else. Where others in my workplace feel inadequate, I'm convinced that I'm overqualified. Where my boss seems to need to hide his weaknesses, I'm convinced that I don't have any weaknesses. Nothing in me, Lord, seeks to sit in the back row. If I'm good at anything, I'm good at proclaiming my accomplishments and at letting my coworkers know all about the amazing things I've accomplished.

I need the strength and wisdom to not do that, God. Help me invite others to speak about themselves, and give me the good sense to just shut up and listen. Amen.

KEEPING MY TEMPER IN CHECK

*A quick-tempered person does foolish things,
and the one who devises evil schemes is hated.*
PROVERBS 14:17

Peace, God, I need peace. I need it because I have learned that the less of it I have, the quicker I am to become angry, and the more likely I am to yell, slam others, and speak poorly about my friends.

And my temper gets the best of me at all the worst possible times—when my boss corrects me, when my wife asks me to change a light bulb, when my children need my attention.

I don't want to be the quick-tempered, always-angry guy others can't stand to be around. Slow down my anger, God. Help me to be calm, to be slower to anger, and to stay away from saying foolish things. Help me instead to honor You with every word that comes out of my mouth. Amen.

DON'T WALK WITH THE WICKED

*Like a muddied spring or a polluted well are
the righteous who give way to the wicked.*
PROVERBS 25:26

I've probably lived this passage one hundred times over,
God. I've surrendered my good, godly life to walk with
wicked people. It's too easy to walk with wicked people.
To be honest, wickedness can be fun and can offer
immediate gratification. But when I walk with wicked
people, I begin to speak and behave as they do. When
that happens, You feel far away.

Lord, guide my decisions as I pick my close friends and
acquaintances. I know there is no way I can completely
avoid associating with those who walk in darkness—not as
long as I live on this earth. But keep me from associating
with the wicked in such a way that I am tempted to walk
as they walk. Amen.

SPEAKING FOR THOSE WHO CANNOT SPEAK

Speak up for those who cannot speak for themselves,
for the rights of all who are destitute.
PROVERBS 31:8

Lord, make me an advocate for those who cannot speak for themselves. Help me to speak for young men who live under the shadow of abuse. Help me to advocate for homeless men in my city. Give me courage to speak for women who are neglected and abused at the hands of angry, sinful men. Give me the courage to stand up for those in my close circle of friends who are buried under mountains of debt, insecurity, grief, and sin. Make me an encourager for these people, a friend who seeks their good at the expense of my own. Make my voice louder than the injustices around me. Amen.

PUNISHING OTHERS

Do not say, "I'll pay you back for this wrong!"
Wait for the Lord, and he will avenge you.
PROVERBS 20:22

Waiting for Your vengeance is difficult, God, and I'd rather just handle things my own way. When someone has wronged me, going after them is much easier than waiting for You to bring about a resolution.

When I unleash my own sense of justice, I feel better. I don't want to hurt others, but I also don't want to let others step all over me or take advantage of me. But, Lord, I know that when I respond to being wronged that way, I am not behaving in a way that glorifies and pleases You.

Lord, I know You don't want me to allow others to take advantage of me or intentionally mistreat me. But I also know that You want me to respond to situations like that with love, not vengeance. Help me to remember that it's Your job, not mine, to handle wrongs that have been done against me. Amen.

SEEKING TO GET RICH

*Do not wear yourself out to get rich;
do not trust your own cleverness.*
PROVERBS 23:4

Lord, as the bills pile up, my kids need school clothes, my friends want me to vacation with them, and my eyes are spying a new car. Living is expensive, God, and living well is *very* expensive.

My choice is fairly simple: I can choose to find a way to live within my means and adopt a heart of gratitude for all You've given me; or I can strive to earn more so that I can purchase those things that I can't presently afford—and honestly don't really need.

Protect my mind, God. Don't allow me to lust after the things I don't need. Teach me wisdom in how to best use the resources You've blessed me with, and prevent me from desiring wealth and riches. Help me keep my eyes focused only on You, and not on the wealth that I think I need. Amen.

ACCEPTING INSTRUCTION

*Those who forsake instruction praise the wicked,
but those who heed it resist them.*
PROVERBS 28:4

Lord, there's an attitude of surrender that comes with being a kingdom person. Being a kingdom person requires that I give up my need to be in control in all situations, and one of the areas where I like to assert my control is in my need to be right all the time.

I know that wisdom comes from listening to others talk about their experiences, from hearing others' stories of success and failure and learning from them. God, teach me never to forsake the instruction of the wise people You've placed in my life. Even more, give me the courage to seek them out and invite them to tell me what they've learned through their own successes and failures. Finally, give me the humility it takes to ask them to critique how I'm living. Amen.

SCRIPTURAL INDEX